PLURALITY AND AMBIGUITY

Plurality And Ambiguity

Hermeneutics, Religion, Hope

David Tracy

1817

Harper & Row, Publishers, San Francisco

New York, Grand Rapids, Philadelphia, St. Louis
London, Singapore, Sydney, Tokyo, Toronto

FIRST HARPER & ROW PAPERBACK EDITION PUBLISHED IN 1989.

Library of Congress Cataloging-in-Publication Data

Tracy, David.
    Plurality and ambiguity.

    Includes index.
    1. Theology—Methodology.   2. Hermeneutics—
Religious aspects—Christianity.   I. Title.
BR118.T68 1987   230′.01′8   85-50248
ISBN 0-06-254742-9
ISBN 0-06-068429-1 (pbk.)

90 91 92 93   RRD   10 9 8 7 6 5 4 3 2

In memory of

my father, John Charles Tracy
my brother, John Charles Tracy, Jr.

Contents

Preface

The theme of this small book is conversation. Perhaps that often neglected but central fact of our intellectual lives may be strengthened by some hard reflection on its possibilities in our post-modern situation. There is no intellectual, cultural, political, or religious tradition of interpretation that does not ultimately live by the quality of its conversation; there is also no tradition that does not eventually have to acknowledge its own plurality and ambiguity.

To face the plurality and ambiguity within conversation involves several questions. Some of these questions have become single chapters of this book. The first question and thus the first chapter is what is conversation and how may it function as a model for all interpretation? Then, in three chapters, the principal problems for that model of conversation are considered. Chapter 2 analyzes how classical modes of argument have become modern theories, methods, and explanations that can interrupt all traditional conversations. Chapter 3 studies a yet more radical interruption of all conversation—that sense of radical plurality disclosed in post-modern studies of language as a disseminating, not a unifying, force. Chapter 4 analyzes the most powerful interruption of all: the radical ambiguity of all conversations in all traditions as a heightened consciousness of the "terror of history" becomes ever more pervasive in the late twentieth century.

At that point in the argument of the book as a whole, chapter 5 argues for the need to reformulate the question of religion as a question of hope. On that reading, post-modern hermeneutics is the test of any interpretation of any religion; at the same time, religion, as the most pluralistic, ambiguous, and important reality of all, is the most difficult and thereby the best test of any theory of interpretation. Such is the central claim of this book. Only the book as a whole and the critical conversation it may provoke—and not any preface to it—can support that claim.

In the future, I hope to write a more strictly theological companion volume to this book that will assess the implications of these reflections on plurality, ambiguity, and hope for interpreting my own Christian tradition. What the "essence of Christianity" might be after Christians seriously acknowledge first, the plurality within their own traditions, second, the import of the many other religious traditions for Christian self-understanding and third, the profound cognitive, moral, and religious ambiguity of Christianity itself is, to put it mildly, a very difficult question—but that is another task for another time, and one helpfully analyzed only in a separate volume.

A work wherein the major model is conversation should be grounded in the practice of many conversations. For myself, one of the few joys left when I reread the final final draft (alas, there were many drafts) were the frequent memories of past conversations evoked by the text. Indeed there are very few worthwhile insights in this work which are not the fruit of such conversation, followed by reflections in solitude, which itself is, as Plato insisted, only another form of conversation.

The places of conversation are also important, both as geographical places and as Aristotelian *topoi:* those places where insight, reflection, and argument may be found. I have been blessed with several such places. First of all, my academic home, the University of Chicago, where serious conversation is more often than not something like a way of life. In the classes and colloquia of the Divinity School, in the seminars of the Committee on the Analysis of Ideas and Methods, as well as many other places at the university, my many friends and colleagues (which certainly includes the students) may, I hope, find in this book their own memories of some of those moments and places at Chicago. I remain deeply thankful to all of them and to our common place of serious conversation, the University of Chicago.

I have tried to extend that conversation by giving parts of this book as lectures (in sometimes greatly altered versions) elsewhere. I am deeply grateful for those opportunities: especially for the Oreon E. Scott lectureship at Phillips University, the Homer J. Armstrong lectureship at Kalamazoo College (and especially to the gracious Dean Robert Dewey), and the Richard Joshua Reynolds lectureship at Emory & Henry Colleges. I also recall, with gratitude, the important reflections of many colleagues at the University of Sewanee; Redlands University; Claremont College; the University of Nevada-Reno; the Philosophical Association of the Philadelphia area meeting at Villanova University; the colloquium of hermeneutics structured by Professor Marco Olivetti at the University of Rome; Mercer University; the Aspen Institute; Emory University; the Woodrow Wilson Center in Washington, D.C.; Trinity College, Dublin; the Jewish-Christian center at Christian Theological Seminary; the University of Tübingen; the Rhetoric Seminar of the American Academy of Religion; my colleagues at the annual meetings of the journal *Concilium;* my colleagues in the seminars on rhetoric, grammar, and religion in the Committee on the Analysis of Ideas & Methods; the generous hospitality and many conversations at Cathedral College, Douglaston. These and several other geographic places have become *topoi* of living conversation. In all of these places I have had the privilege to discuss some of these ideas in different forms and forums.

Indeed in other versions a few parts of this book have found another kind of home in such publications as *The Proceedings* of the Catholic Theological Society of America, *The Proceedings* for the International Colloquium on Hermeneutics at the University of Rome and the papers for the symposium on "Religion and Intellectual Life in America" of the Woodrow Wilson Center. To all of them, my profound and enduring thanks.

Many friends and colleagues have also generously given me their reflections on different sections of earlier drafts of this text. There is no question in my mind that it is a better text because of their reflections. There is also little doubt that the text could be an even better one if I had listened more carefully to their observations. At the inevitable and painful risk of forgetting others, let me recall some to whom I am especially indebted: Adriana Berger, James Buchanan, Hugh Corrigan, Joseph Edelheit, Franklin Gamwell, Langdon Gilkey, Andrew Greeley, Bradford Hinze, Robert Jones, Eugene Kennedy, Steven Kepnes, Joseph Komonchak, Mary Knutsen, Martin Marty, Katrina McLeod, Wendy Doniger O'Flaherty, Paul Ricoeur, Susan Shapiro, Tod Swanson, and William Warthling. The list may seem long but in fact is far too short to express adequate thanks to all. I am thankful as well to the prodding and patience of my editor, Justus George Lawler, and to the anonymous but properly fierce copyeditors at Harper & Row.

Finally, special thanks go to several persons who endured with patience and firmness several drafts of this book. First, to my two research assistants over the last two years, Charles Allen and Stephen Webb, for their many labors as well as their many helpful and critical suggestions. Second, to my mother Eileen Tracy Couch, for her criticisms and her tireless typing, the latter aided at crucial moments by Judith Lawrence. Then, to my friends and colleagues, Mary Gerhart, David Grene, and David Smigelskis, for their critical aid in helping me rethink my positions and thus rewrite the text at crucial moments; further thanks to Mary Gerhart for her excellent index. Fourth, to my friend and colleague, Peter Bartlett, who, when I thought I was finally finished, took me through a two-month exercise which every writer both longs for and dreads—a complete rewriting of the book for greater clarity and brevity: whatever was not clear must be totally rewritten; whatever was merely repetitious must go. Peter Bartlett's demanding standards have rendered this work both shorter and I hope clearer. My deep thanks to all.

A central theme of this book is memory. That theme recalls for me, with pain but with a gratitude I can never adequately repay, the recent deaths of two mentors and friends whose persons and work have deeply enriched my life: Mircea Eliade and Bernard Lonergan. I hope that some readers of this small book may be encouraged to read the great works of Eliade and Lonergan.

I remember, as well, with thanks and with gratitude, my father, John Charles Tracy, and by brother, John Charles Tracy, Jr.—to both of whose memory this book is dedicated.

Chicago, September 10, 1986

CHAPTER 1

Interpretation, Conversation, Argument

In January 1983 the Polish director Ardrzej Wajda released a film on the French Revolution entitled *Danton*. Despite Wajda's objections, many interpreted the film as an allegory of the Solidarity movement in Poland. Was the gregarious, self-indulgent, patriotic, admirable Danton in the film really Lech Walesa? Was the neat, neurotic, unbending Robespierre in the film really General Jaruselski? To watch the film with a Polish audience is to learn from their reactions that many scenes, whether intentionally or not, cannot but yield double meanings. Wajda may have been correct to resist the too easy allegorical reading of Danton = Walesa and Robespierre = Jaruselski. Still, the metaphors in the film evoke present and past Polish history; indeed, the double meanings proved too resonant for most audiences to resist.

Many French intellectuals, however, found the resonances not merely resistible but insulting. The film became a cause célèbre around which the classic French debate on how to interpret the great Revolution erupted once again. Much of the socialist left was enraged by the film. Had not historical scholarship since at least the time of Mathiez destroyed the earlier republican and liberal applause for Danton and enshrined Robespierre as the true hero of the Revolution? Had the Pole Wajda, obsessed with his own country's crisis, dared to tamper with their Revolution? The debate intensified as it became known that the film had been partly sponsored by the French government itself as a kind of overture to the forthcoming celebration of the bicentennial of the Revolution. The president, François Mitterand, shared the dis-

tress of his fellow socialists, especially when it became clear that
the younger generations, while enjoying the film, seemed untroubled by their elders' debates over Danton or Robespierre.
He called a special cabinet meeting to demand a study of how
French history was being taught in the schools. But it soon became clear that the historians themselves were deeply divided.
The avant-garde historians did not believe in analyzing, much
less evaluating, what traditional historians concentrate on, that
is, events, politics, and personalities. For them, analyses of long-
range geographical, climatic, demographic, and social realities
were the central tasks of the modern historian, even an historian
of that too easily ideologized and romanticized event, *the* Revolution. But President Mitterand, who is known to keep a copy
of Michelet by his bedside, would insist: yet another reform of
the teaching of history in French schools must begin. The young
must learn the correct view of the Revolution so that they would
be able to choose between Danton and Robespierre—and on
French, not Polish, grounds.[1]

The French Revolution—what was it?[2] The beginning of the
modern age or merely the continuation of traditional power politics by other means? Michelet's stirring portrait of a "religion of
humanity" created by a people at last free of oppression? Carlyle's apocalyptic saga, where the event destroyed every individual it touched? Taine's phantasmagoric portrayal of the sheer
insanity of events, of the corrupting of all the groups and individuals involved? The careful and well-nigh established Marxist reading of Lefebvre and Soboul, where a feudal caste yielded
to a bourgeois democracy that, in its turn, successfully resisted
the emergence of a true people's democracy? The revisionary
republican interpretations of Furet, based on new historical
methods designed to analyze the conflict of political discourses?
The classic interruptive event of early modernity praised by such
diverse contemporaries of the event as Kant, Goethe, Fichte,
Hegel, Wordsworth, Blake, Paine, and Jefferson? The interruptive event denounced by Burke and all those who followed him,
including the later Wordsworth and Fichte? The controlling
power of events over human life captured in the narratives of
Dickens and Balzac? The continuation of certain fundamental
social tendencies of the ancien régime classically analyzed by de
Tocqueville? A single moment in a larger "Atlantic revolution"—

Holland, England, Ireland, the United States—of Palmer and Godechot? A surface of events and ideas beneath which irresistible social, economic, and even geographic forces were in control? A moment where the conflicting ideas of Rousseau, Voltaire, Diderot, and Montesquieu were genuinely at stake? Or was the Revolution no single event at all, but rather a series of heterogeneous events connected by no easily decipherable causal links? A series of events constituted by individual ideologies, temperaments, and idiosyncrasies joined to chance and luck? A series of events whose interpretation will not yield to the grand generalizations of Michelet, Carlyle, or Taine or even of Jaurès, Aulard, and Mathiez but demands a series of more modest scholarly events: solid monographs based on the archival research into all the available resources on some one aspect of some one event in the great Revolution?

To a nonspecialist like myself, the debates among historians of the French Revolution present one of the most compelling examples of the difficulty of interpreting any classic event or any classic text, symbol, ritual, or person. Whether reactionary, conservative, liberal-republican, socialist or communist, we are direct descendants of the debates and struggles among the émigrés, the aristocratic reformers, the Girondins, the Dantonists, the Jacobins, the Hébertists. Despite their many differences, both Mitterand and Wajda share one crucial insight: if we are to understand ourselves and our postmodern situation, we must risk interpreting that revolution which inaugurated the modern world. The scholarly debates on that palimpsest of events we too easily call the French Revolution continue unabated, for that event still affects us.

We know, as clearly as did the contemporaries of the Revolution, that something epoch-making happened—affecting not only the history of France, indeed not only the history of the West, but, as the present struggles in the Third World testify, the entire world. Was the Russian Revolution the completion of the French, or its betrayal? Are the present Western democracies the legitimate heirs of the Revolution or the heirs of the Thermidorean reaction? Are the struggles for social and political liberation in the Third World, as well as the struggles, as Wajda insists, in the Second World, the true descendants of the Revolution, or its caricature?

Interpreters interested in how to trace the history of effects of any classic event need only recall the continuing conflictual receptions, in both theory and practice, of the French Revolution. Interpreters anxious to search for the causes of historical events need only follow the debates of the historians:[3] the historians, still divided between geographic, social, demographic, economic, and political analyses; divided anew by traditional historical narratives on events, ideas, and persons and modern analyses of ethnography, structures, and *mentalités*; ideologically still divided between the "thesis of circumstances" of the left and the "thesis of conspiracy" of the right. Anyone attempting to know just how difficult it is to interpret any classic event, symbol, text, ritual, ideology, or person need recall only the basic outlines of each in the great Revolution.

How can we adequately interpret any single event, much less the possible causal relationships among them? The aristocratic revolt of 1787–88; the calling of the Estates-General; the tennis court oath; the peasant uprisings; the fall of the Bastille; the march on Versailles; the flight to Varennes; the emergence of the clubs, especially the Jacobins; the assault on the Tuileries; the September Massacres; the uprisings of the Vendée; conscription and war; the trial and execution of the king; the reaction of the other European powers; the battle of Valmy; the Terror; the events of Thermidor and the Directory; the events of Brumaire and the triumph of Bonaparte?

How should we interpret the texts of the Revolution? Predecessor texts like the works of Rousseau, Montesquieu, and the philosophes; anticipatory texts like the American Declaration of Independence and the Constitution; contemporary texts such as Abbé Sieyès's *What Is the Third Estate?*; the pamphlets of Marat, Desmoulins, and Hébert; the different constitutions drafted, accepted, or rejected; the Declaration of the Rights of Man and Citizen; conflicting foreign interpretations such as the classics of Edmund Burke and Thomas Paine?

How can we analyze adequately the new symbols of the Revolution? The Marseillaise and the *ça ira*; the sansculottes of legend and fact; the cap of liberty and Marianne; the King of France become the king of the French only to end as Citizen Capet; the attempt to replace the formal *vous* by the more egalitarian *tu*; the new republican calendar; the queen, Marie Antoinette, become the widow Capet; the Bastille, the Conciergerie, the shuttered and empty Versailles; the tributes to ancient republican Rome—interpreted in one way by Danton's use of Voltaire's idealized portrait of sensual, democratic Athens, interpreted in quite another way by Robespierre's use of Rousseau's equally idealized portrait of virtuous, ascetic Sparta; the Arcadian shepherdess in the paintings of Fragonard yielding to the Spartan heroes in the paintings of David; the barricades, the tumbrils, and the guillotine; the Republic of Virtue become the Terror ("Terror without virtue is blind; virtue without terror is impotent")?

What kind of ideological analysis can provide a just account of the aims, achievements, and failures of the various groups and movements? The émigrés, the aristocratic reformers, the republicans of '89, the Girondins, Jacobins, Indulgents, Hébertists, the Directory?

Who can adequately interpret the individuals in the Revolution, individuals whom no novelist could invent and no biographer exhaust? Louis XVI, Marie Antoinette, Necker, Mirabeau, Lafayette, Brissot, Marat, Charlotte Corday, Bailly, Madame Roland, Fouquier-Tinville, Philippe Égalité, Condorcet, Fouché, Doctor Guillotin, Madame du Barry, Talleyrand, Desmoulins, Danton, the Dauphin, Pius VI, Couthon, Saint-Just, Robespierre, Barras, Carnot, Sieyès, Bonaparte?

How can studies of ritual illuminate the ritualistic aspects of the Revolution? The anticlimactic release of seven prisoners from the Bastille; the insatiable fury of the September Massacres; the swearing in of the constitutional clergy in the *Champ de Mars* presided over by the ultimate survivor, Talleyrand; the feast of the Supreme Being presided over by the "sea-green incorruptible" Robespierre; the feast of Reason in Notre Dame; the drums drowning out the king's final words at the guillotine; the destruction of the royal tombs at Saint-Denis and of much else now judged feudal, gothic, oppressive; the bizarre spectacle of the trial and beheading of the corpse of the long-dead Richelieu; the procession of the tumbrils to the guillotine; the seemingly endless parade of pitiable individuals undergoing the new public ritual of death?

The events, texts, symbols, movements, individuals, rituals multiply. And below and within them lie those discourses, structures, and *mentalités* that the new historians have taught us to search for. All demand attention in the quest for an adequate interpretation of the Revolution.

The debate on the causes of the Revolution continues. So too does the debate on its effects. Consider the years 1815, 1830, 1848, 1870, 1917, or, closer to our own times, 1968. Like the singular years 1789 and 1848, 1968 can haunt our memories with revolutionary hopes both released and shattered: in Paris itself, the May events; in the United States, the marches and riots in the cities, the assassinations of Martin Luther King, Jr., and Robert Kennedy; in Mexico City, the massacre of the students; in Medellin, the hope expressed in the liberation conference of the Latin American bishops; in Czechoslovakia, Soviet tanks crushing "socialism with a human face." All these events are also part of the history of effects of the great Revolution, as is the Solidarity movement, as indeed is anyone likely to be reading this book at all.

The historical questions on the Revolution continue. Was it true, as de Tocqueville believed, that "never was any such event so inevitable yet so completely unforeseen"? Who were the sans-culottes? What was the role of the peasants in the Great Fear, in the Vendée, and in their relationship to the cities? Was the death of the king inevitable? Did external invasion and internal civil war cause the Terror? Was Robespierre a Machiavellian or an idealist or some curious combination of both? What role did the Duke of Orléans play? Was Gracchus Babeuf a forerunner of Lenin? Was the Terror the first experiment in modern totalitarianism? Was the Revolution a class struggle? Was it a revolution of aristocratic demands? of bourgeois hopes? of the people? Who were the people? Was the Revolution caused more by deficits and bad harvests or by rising expectations? Was it a revolution of lawyers? How much support did the counterrevolutionary forces actually have? What was the role of the clergy? How Parisian was the Revolution? What role did the clubs and the Paris populace play in the deliberation of the various assemblies? What really changed? Why France? Was anyone in control? How great a part did ideas and ideologies actually have in shaping events? Was the de-Christianization campaign necessary? Would matters have been very different with a stronger king? Or if Mirabeau had lived? Or if Danton had prevailed? Or if Robespierre had survived? Were the conversations in the salons responsible for the arguments in the Committee on Public Safety? Was the Directory a betrayal of the Revolution? Was Napoleon?

The answers to all these questions remain open. But the major question for any contemporary interpreter reflecting on the history of effects of the Revolution inevitably shifts to the question, What is the French Revolution now? What is that Revolution to us, its later narrators, analysts, and heirs? Can any of us claim to know how to reconcile individual liberty with equality, reason with tradition, the continuities of history with its radical interruptions? Like all serious questioning of all classic events, texts, symbols, rituals, and persons, the question, What is the French Revolution? soon becomes the demand, Who are we, we uneasy postmodern heirs of this pluralistic and ambiguous heritage? What was the French Revolution?

At times, interpretations matter. On the whole, such times are times of cultural crisis. The older ways of understanding and practice, even experience itself, no longer seem to work. We can find ourselves distanced from all earlier ways. Then we need to reflect on what it means to interpret. We find that in order to understand at all we must interpret. We may even find that to understand we need to interpret the very process of understanding-as-interpretation. Such moments can occur readily enough in any individual's life. The great creative individuals—thinkers, artists, heroes, saints—found themselves impelled to find new ways to interpret an experience that their culture or tradition seemed unable to interpret well or even at all. For Luther, for example, this happened when he first discovered Paul and, through Paul, himself. Euripides, drawn as he was to the tragic forms and visions of Aeschylus and Sophocles, could not interpret reality in their way or with their forms.

And yet, important as reflection on unusual individuals is, the larger crisis is likely to be elsewhere: in a tradition, a culture, or a language that can no longer simply move forward by means of its usual ways of experiencing, understanding, acting, or interpreting. Luther found himself confronted by the radical crisis of late medieval German society. Euripides was caught up in the political crisis of Athenian democracy and empire as well as the intellectual crisis of the Sophistic and Socratic intellectual revolutions. The later Roman Stoics found themselves in a postheroic culture distanced from the Homeric and Athenian pasts and needing to find new ways of interpreting them. Indeed, the Stoics, like the Jewish and Christian allegorizers, found a need to reflect on the process of interpretation itself in order to understand at all.

A crisis of interpretation within any tradition eventually becomes a demand to interpret this very process of interpretation. Philo and Augustine, Descartes and Spinoza, Hegel and Schleiermacher, Peirce and Wittgenstein experienced the same kind of hermeneutic crisis in which we now find ourselves. But who is this "we"? We are those Westerners shaped by the seventeenth-century scientific revolution, the eighteenth-century Enlightenment, and the nineteenth-century industrial revolution and explosion of historical consciousness. We late-twentieth-century Westerners find ourselves in a century where human-made mass death has been practiced, where yet another technological revolution is occurring, where global catastrophe or even extinction could occur. We find ourselves unable to proceed as if all that had not happened, is not happening, or could not happen. We find ourselves historically distanced from the classics of our traditions. We find ourselves culturally distanced from those "others" we have chosen both to ignore and oppress. We find ourselves distanced even from ourselves, suspicious of all our former ways of understanding, interpreting, and acting.

All of us know we have been formed by traditions whose power impinges upon us both consciously and preconsciously. We now begin to glimpse the profound plurality and ambiguity of our traditions. As Westerners we have also become conscious of those other traditions whose power we sense, but whose meaning for us we do not yet begin to know how to interpret. We find ourselves impelled by the same kind of hermeneutic urgency as Augustine in late classical antiquity or Schleiermacher and Hegel in early modernity. Like them, we need to find new ways of interpreting ourselves and our traditions. Like them, we may even find ourselves compelled to reflect on the very process of understanding as interpretation.

Interpretation is a lifelong project for any individual in any culture. But only in times of cultural crisis does the question of interpretation itself become central. At such times it may be enough to recall the famous Chinese curse: may you live in "interesting times." We need to reflect on what none of us can finally evade: the need to interpret in order to understand at all.

Interpretation seems a minor matter, but it is not. Every time we act, deliberate, judge, understand, or even experience, we are interpreting. To understand at all is to interpret. To act well is to interpret a situation demanding some action and to interpret a correct strategy for that action. To experience in other than a purely passive sense (a sense less than human) is to interpret; and to be "experienced" is to have become a good interpreter. Interpretation is thus a question as unavoidable, finally, as experience, understanding, deliberation, judgment, decision, and action.[4] To be human is to act reflectively, to decide deliberately, to understand intelligently, to experience fully. Whether we know it or not, to be human is to be a skilled interpreter.

We admittedly cannot offer a fully explicit account of the complex human skill of interpreting any more than we could offer such an account of any one of our other practical skills. Nevertheless, studying a variety of models for understanding this central but puzzling phenomenon can aid us in developing the practices necessary for good interpreters: those that enrich our experience, allow for understanding, aid deliberation and judgment, and increase the possibilities of meaningful action. It is, of course, possible—in some cases even desirable—to avoid those explicit reflections on interpretation named interpretation theory. But with careful attention, and with some reflection on what we already do, anyone can also learn interpretation theories (or hermeneutics). Then we may use these theories as they should be used: as further practical skills for the central task of becoming human. In turning to interpretation theory we are simply following Kenneth Burke's fine dictum: "Use all that can be used."[5]

All theory of interpretation—like all theory itself—is an interpretation as good or as bad as its ability to illuminate the problems we discover or invent and its ability to increase the possibilities of good action. Good theory, after all, is both an abstraction from, and an enrichment of, our concrete experience. Theory necessarily abstracts from actual practice to highlight certain salient, sometimes essential, but never exhaustive features of that practice. When theory works well, it provides a plausible interpretation of some essential features of a puzzling phenomenon of practice. Then abstraction enriches all practice and thought by helping us understand some features of reality that it would be wise to keep in mind. But if theory attempts to displace skill and understanding in concrete situations, it becomes first a nuisance and later a hindrance to both thought and action. Then it deserves to be thrown on the pile of "mere" theories. Hermeneutical theories, like any other theories, can merit that fate, but they can just as easily become helpful skills forged on behalf of thought and life.

Such, we hope, is the case with the present interest across the disciplines in hermeneutics. Such is surely the case when hermeneutical theory is used to illuminate our common problems in ways related to, because tested and transformed by, concrete practices. Practice itself is often as good or as bad as the interpretation it uses and ultimately is. The reintroduction of the word *praxis* into the English language, for example, serves a useful practical function. From the side of the theoreticians, our familiar word *practice* is too often understood as mere practice, the simple application of all too pure and contextless theories. From the side of the practitioners, practice can become a desperate cry for an illusory freedom from the interpretations and theories that all practice counsciously or unconsciously involves. The word *praxis,* however, by its very strangeness in English, reminds us that every worthwhile practice is informed by some theory. *Praxis* can also remind us that theoretical activity is itself a praxis—and one to be tested by the practice it serves. If we need to remind ourselves of these central facts of intellectual life, then by all means let us use the word *praxis* to do so. One day, the preferable words *practice* and *skill* will return to our language use, for then they will return freed of current prejudice.

We may begin the process of interpreting interpretation by starting with what seems obvious if indeterminate. Any act of interpretation involves at least three realities: some phenomenon to be interpreted, someone interpreting that phenomenon, and some interaction between these first two realities.[6] How can we understand, that is, interpret, these three facts? That, at a first level of reflection, is the problem of interpretation.

In order to avoid the temptations to pure subjectivity, it is better to start not with the interpreter but with the phenomenon requiring interpretation. This phenomenon can be literally anything: a law, an action, a ritual, a symbol, a text, a person, an event. Think again of interpreting the French Revolution; it demands attention to all these phenomena. Any of these possibilities is a good test case of understanding-as-interpretation. But as Kant reminds us with his distinction between a mere instance and an example, one of the most crucial moves in any attempt to understand is to find a good example, one which does exemplify the question at issue.

To search for the illuminating example, in everyday life as in scientific inquiry, is to search for a good test case for concrete understanding. How can we understand what could be other than it is? How can we understand, on any particular question, which possibilities have been verified and why? How can we understand which assertions are warranted and by what criteria? How can we understand the contingent? How can we render the indeterminate more determinate? One crucial move for all such inquiry, as Aristotle insists in both the *Rhetoric* and the *Topics*, is to search for and test the right example, the best test case of the phenomenon we seek to understand.[7]

Modern hermeneutics since Schleiermacher may have been correct to concentrate on the example of written texts. Why? First, in literate cultures, written texts have played a central role. Second, when literate cultures are in crisis, the crisis is most evident in the question of what they do with their exemplary written texts. What happens, for example, in those religious communities whose scriptural texts have been affected by historical consciousness and its inevitable companion, a sense of historical distance? What happens in secular cultures when their written texts, named classics, begin to unravel under the impact of this same historical consciousness? What happens when the canon of accepted texts is overthrown, as it was in China's cultural revolution? What happens when cultural parochialism becomes evident to the culture itself? What happens when an event like the Holocaust erupts in the culture?

Written texts seem to provide stability for literate cultures. At the same time, written texts are exposed to great instability when intellectual and moral crisis occurs. This combination of stability and instability renders written texts a good example of the inner complexity of any phenomenon requiring interpretation. Other phenomena such as oral traditions, social practices, and historical events seem more obviously unstable than written texts. They are more clearly open to endless revisionary interpretations. Other phenomena such as some symbols or hardened social practices can often seem so permanent as to be almost second nature. They seem to display a greater stability than written texts. Yet the latter in fact provide a good example of the transience affecting all phenomena. "What goes without saying" is what seems so stable but never is.

In recent years we have come a long way from the now old New Criticism's belief in the stability of an autonomous text. We are in the midst of a deconstructive drive designed to expose the radical instability of all texts and the inevitable intertextuality of all seemingly autonomous texts. The once stable author has been replaced by the unstable reader. Written texts seem, commonsensically, stable enough. But when we reflect on any effort to understand them by interpreting them, they begin to seem far more puzzling and unstable than we first might have imagined.

To understand the concrete, we always need good examples. Among good examples, some stand out as paradigmatic. Among good examples of written texts, the truly exemplary ones are named classics.[8] The classics, therefore, are exemplary examples. As such, they are a good test case for any interpretation theory. On historical grounds, classics are simply those texts that have helped found or form a particular culture. On more explicitly hermeneutical grounds, classics are those texts that bear an excess and permanence of meaning, yet always resist definitive interpretation. In their production, there is also the following paradox: though highly particular in origin and expression, classics have the possibility of being universal in their effect. Moreover, in their continuing reception, which is what ultimately counts for any hermeneutical theory, another paradox is evident. Their ability as classics can be culturally dependent upon the instability of the particular culture's shifting canon of classics.[9] For in any particular period some classics will disappear from the canon while others, once forgotten or even repressed, will reappear.

In the eighteenth century, the Roman classics played a major canonical role. With the romantic movement, the Greeks returned, and the Romans retreated. Compare, for example, the role of the Roman classics for the eighteenth-century Whigs with the role of the Greek classics for their nineteenth-century descendants, Athens for the Victorians, Homer for the Edwardians.[10] In German culture, recall the role of the Roman classics for Kant, with the refrain from Hegel through Heidegger that we Germans *are* the Greeks. The American Revolutionaries dressed themselves in the robes of republican Rome, whereas Robespierre chose Sparta to interpret the Romans. Contrast Houdon's Roman statue of Washington with David's Spartan painting of the assassinated Marat. In American culture the early republic's obsession with Rome later yielded, in the midst of civil war and romantic upheaval, to Lincoln's new interpretation. When we now read Jefferson's Declaration of Independence, we are likely to read it through Lincoln's eyes rather than Jefferson's. Indeed, so much is this the case that Lincoln's biblical reading, in effect, determined a second founding of the American ideal of the republic.

The biblical texts have exercised a similar role throughout Western history. On the whole, the Scriptures have served, as Northrop Frye insists, as a kind of great code for Western culture.[11] And yet this code has functioned with extraordinary flexibility. Consider, for example, the role of Paul's letter to the Romans before and after Luther or, more recently, before and after the belated twentieth-century Christian discovery of rabbinic exegesis.[12] Consider the retrieval of kabbalistic readings of Genesis after the expulsion of Spanish Jewry. Or notice the conflictual history of interpretation of apocalyptic texts in both Christian and secular movements from Joachim of Fiore through Hegel and Marx to political and liberation theology. Mark's Gospel, once so clear, stable, and slightly boring—'and then Jesus said, and then he went, and then he did'—has become in the last few years a strangely modernist document filled with interruptions, reversals, and uncanny nonendings. Luke-Acts is still received in conflicting ways by very different Christian groups: charismatics appealing to the role of the Spirit in these texts, liberation and political theologians insisting upon the preferential option for the poor, liberal Christians content with Luke's rather commonsensical account of Jesus, Barthians anxious to show how

Luke resembles a nineteenth-century realistic novel rendering the true identity of the main character through its historylike narrative.[13]

John's Gospel will always appeal to the contemplatives, mystics, metaphysicians, and theologians of any Christian tradition. Yet this Gospel too has been received in different ways—so different that they remain difficult to trace with anything like adequacy. Matthew will always find a receptive audience in Christian communities intent on community life, from the descendants of the radical wing of the Reformation, such as the Mennonites, the Amish, and the Church of the Brethren, to descendants of Tridentine Catholicism.

There is, in fact, no classic text that has not occasioned the same kind of puzzling history of reception.[14] And later readers cannot but come to these texts with the sometimes conscious, more often preconscious, memories of those former readings. No classic text comes to us either pure or autonomous. Every classic bears with it the history of its own conflictual history of reception. Indeed, every classic brings a history of effects that we can never fully explicate. Every classic bears its own permanence and excess of meaning. But its permanence can quickly become excess. And that excess can sometimes yield to a radical instability of different receptions that defy any definitive interpretation. The history of the interpretation of any classic is indeed a curious phenomenon. But that history is repeated in every culture's reading of its classic texts.

The cultural phenomenon of the classic text, therefore, demands some hermeneutical reflection on what a classic is. This is not the case merely because the classics play so formative and transformative a role for every culture. Scholars do not own the classics any more than traditionalists own the traditions that form our cultural lives. The classic is important hermeneutically because it represents the best exemplar of what we seek: an example of both radical stability become permanence and radical instability become excess of meaning through ever-changing receptions. The classic texts are not unique; they are merely the best examples for testing any theory of interpretation because they are the most puzzling examples of the complex process of interpretation itself.

There is yet another reason why classic texts can serve an

exemplary function for the modern problem of hermeneutics: the claim to attention of the classics is difficult to ignore. To encourage interaction between text and interpreter, it is helpful to find examples where the interpreter is forced to recognize otherness by confronting an unexpected claim to truth. So immune can we all become to otherness that we are tempted to reduce all reality to more of the same or to that curious substitute for the same we too often mean when we say similarity.[15] It is difficult to approach any classic text and force it into the Procrustean bed of more of the same or the deceptively more modest claim that "Well, it is similar enough to what I already know to merit no great effort at understanding."

We can drift half-asleep through nonclassic period pieces. We cannot with the classics. Indeed, the temptation to domesticate all reality is a temptation that any classic text will resist. The classics resist our engrained laziness and self-satisfaction. Their claim to attention must be heeded if understanding is not to slide into either domesticating similarity or mere sameness.

Scholars, to be sure, have their own domesticating impulses that can corral the classics as private property yielding only to their proper readings. Yet, as the great classical interpreters have always recognized, the classics will not be so easily tamed.[16] We may risk identifying with them only at the price of finding our present self-identity undone. We can make them an elite preserve only by repressing their radical otherness and difference from our usual canons of civility. Sophocles is far more frightening than Victorian legends of his sublime cheerfulness allowed. Brecht made some less obvious classics—Villon and Gay—live anew through his attack on bourgeois veneration for the classics. Nietzsche's assault on the preferred reading of the origins of Greek tragedy freed the radical otherness of those great texts. Kierkegaard's insistence on the otherness of the Christian gospel threw "a bomb into the playground of the theologians." In our own period, the power of the biblical texts is often best found in the readings from the basic communities of the poor and marginalized.

Classics, whether texts, symbols, events, persons, or rituals, command attention. As reception theory has clarified, that attention may range all the way from a radical identification with the claim to truth of the classic to some tentative, even hesitant, resonance with its otherness. The classics arrive with powerful claims to attention, yet their claim is, after all, a claim to our attention and a challenge to our usual expectations. We should not become passive recipients of classic possibilities or Don Juans of possibility itself. We are those seeking for truth by risking our present standards in an interpretation of the claim to attention of the classics. In this effort to understand, we become persons capable of recognizing the otherness of the classic. To understand these texts at all is inevitably to understand them differently from how their original authors or their first audiences understood them.[17] Any contemporary interpreter enters the process of interpretation with some preunderstanding of the questions addressed by a classic text. The good interpreter is willing to put that preunderstanding at risk by allowing the classic to question the interpreter's present expectations and standards. That preunderstanding cannot but function in some interaction between text and interpreter. Every interpreter comes to the text bearing those complex histories of effects we call traditions. There is no more a possibility of escape from tradition than there is the possibility of an escape from history or language. No individual reader is any more autonomous than the classic text is.

Anyone who uses a language bears the preunderstandings, partly conscious, more often preconscious, of the traditions of that language. The Enlightenment belief in a purely autonomous consciousness has been as torn apart as Pentheus in the *Bacchae*.[18] If the self is not to become a purely passive carrier of whatever codes—familial, social, historical—have formed it, then every self must risk interpretation. No one can any longer constitute a self through the construction of that Potemkin village, the Cartesian ego, or even that more modest but now-abandoned cottage orné, the Enlightenment version of the autonomous ego. The self finds itself by risking an interpretation of all the signs, symbols, and texts of its own and other cultures. The ego continually constructs a self only by deconstructing all false notions of autonomous identity. Autonomy is a mirrored mask that, ripped away, reveals Narcissus peering at an indecipherable code, believing all the while that he has at last found his true self.

The classic text reaches out through its history of effects to be received by another interpreter in another time. The interpreter reaches out through some preunderstanding and some expectations to the classic text.[19] The text and the interpreter interact. There is no choice as to whether interpreter and text will interact. But how do we understand that peculiar interaction?

To name the heart of this process of interaction as interpretation by the word *game* may seem too lighthearted a description.[20] And yet the peculiar kinds of interactions called games are phenomena worth puzzling about. Every interaction includes some movement. A game enhances that interaction by emphasizing that the movement itself must take over if there is to be a game at all. To play a game demands that I be willing to allow the movement peculiar to this particular game to take over. Even rules are there to assist the game's movement and to restore it when it begins to break down. The players are there not to play their own game, but to lose their usual self-consciousness in the movement of the play itself. The object put into play (the ball, the cards, etc.) is there to actualize the unique kind of interaction in this particular game.

It is not so strange, after all, that Albert Camus claimed that he learned his ethics playing soccer as a boy in Algeria.[21] The sense of freedom and ethical fairness peculiar to some games is at the same time a sense of allowing oneself to experience the demands of the rhythm of the play. If we were doomed to play only those games that Ervin Goffman has described, we would be caught in the trap of "games people play."[22] But if we allow some claim upon our attention from any game, whether through natural or artificial means—the surf, the ball, the boat, the cards, the garden—then we can free ourselves from ourselves, however briefly. We can learn again to play. In some games we, like Rilke, may even be fortunate enough to begin to sense our resonance with the play of the cosmos itself.[23]

And yet, outside the freedom of Watteau's fêtes, Wordsworth's Lake Country, and Cooper's wilderness, or even outside the supremely natural games of the Taoist retreat and the Zen garden, we can all learn to play again. Watch infants or animals at play; they instinctively understand when to let go and simply play.

The movement should free the players from their usual self-consciousness. Think how easily a performance is destroyed if the acting is self-conscious. That same movement should structure the discipline required by the rules of the game. Games liberate our ability to understand ourselves by facing something different, other, and sometimes strange. We can let go of the everyday refusal to play—like Borges with his aleatory games of chance and Nabokov with his favorite game of chess.

Conversation itself is another kind of game. It is a game where we learn to give in to the movement required by questions worth exploring. The movement in conversation is questioning itself. Neither my present opinions on the question nor the text's original response to the question, but the question itself, must control every conversation. A conversation is a rare phenomenon, even for Socrates. It is not a confrontation. It is not a debate. It is not an exam. It is questioning itself. It is a willingness to follow the question wherever it may go. It is dia-logue.[24]

In its original sense, a conversation is of course modeled on an interaction between two or more individuals. When we think of classic conversations, we are likely to think of the dialogues in Plato's academy or the conversation in the salons and coffeehouses of Enlightenment Europe. We are less likely to think of the Café Voltaire in Zurich during World War I as a place where conversation, as opposed to argument or even violence, could take place. When no question other than our own is allowed, then conversation is impossible. Who does not share Stoppard's pleasure in the idea that Joyce, Lenin, and Tristan Tzara actually met?[25] Who can imagine that they could have conversed if they ever met at the Café Voltaire? How frequently does conversation occur in an academic seminar? Less frequently, surely, than in late-night conversations with friends. In any of the classic *topoi* of conversation, questioning takes place. We may pursue conversation with the seriousness of Socrates and Gorgias, with the deftness of Voltaire and Madame du Deffand, or with the rigor of a modern German seminar on the conditions of possibility of conversation itself. We learn to play the game of conversation when we allow questioning to take over. We learn when we allow the question to impose its logic, its demands, and ultimately its own rhythm upon us.

When human beings converse, they may converse, of course, about themselves.[26] They may exchange their narratives, expose their hopes, desires, and fears. They may both reveal and conceal who they think they are, and who they think the other may be—the other now become the conversation partner. But in this kind of conversation, as in any conversation where the subject matter is allowed to take over, we can experience Aristotle's dictum that in the pursuit of truth, friendship must yield. His dictum is all the more striking, coming as it does from the thinker who, more than anyone writing today, insisted upon the difficult demands of that reality we call friendship.[27] Conversation is a game with some hard rules:[28] say only what you mean; say it as accurately as you can; listen to and respect what the other says, however different or other; be willing to correct or defend your opinions if challenged by the conversation partner; be willing to argue if necessary, to confront if demanded, to endure necessary conflict, to change your mind if the evidence suggests it. These are merely some generic rules for questioning. As good rules, they are worth keeping in mind in case the questioning does begin to break down. In a sense they are merely variations of the transcendental imperatives elegantly articulated by Bernard Lonergan: "Be attentive, be intelligent, be responsible, be loving, and, if necessary, change."[29]

We converse with one another. We can also converse with texts. If we read well, then we are conversing with the text. No human being is simply a passive recipient of texts. We inquire. We question. We converse. Just as there is no purely autonomous text, so too there is no purely passive reader. There is only that interaction named conversation.

Whenever we allow the text to have some claim upon our attention, we find that we are never pure creators of meaning. In conversation we find ourselves by losing ourselves in the questioning provoked by the text. We find ourselves by allowing claims upon our attention, by exploring possibilities suggested by others, including those others we call texts. If we want to converse with the author, that is another conversation. But we must realize that the text and the author are not interchangeable. As any author knows, once a text is written, it is on its own. The author has become one more reader. The strange sense of disappointment that we may experience in meeting authors is primarily our problem, not theirs. Once a text exists, we should question the text, and not the author's biography, for its meaning. It was Proust who insisted that art is produced by some self distinct from the self of the everyday life. Indeed, it is suggestive to think that the great artists are able to converse with both forces and questions that most of us shun, repress, or simply are unaware of.

Any claim to the pure autonomy of the text will not survive any good reading. Any claim that the reader creates the text will soon dissolve into sterile return of the same insight in every text. To interact with classic texts is to converse with difference and otherness. There are, as suggested above, some generic rules for good conversation. But there is only one way to understand what the rules are there for: we must insist upon the act of questioning. We must allow that act to test, form, and transform itself by allowing ourselves to question. To understand is to interpret. To interpret is to converse. To converse with any classic text is to find oneself caught up in the questions and answers worthy of a free mind.

Conversation in its primary form is an exploration of possibilities in the search for truth. In following the track of any question, we must allow for difference and otherness. At the same time, as the question takes over, we notice that to attend to the other as other, the different as different, is also to understand the different *as* possible. To recognize possibility is to sense some similarity to what we have already experienced or understood. But similarity here must be described as similarity-in-difference, that is, analogy. An imagination trained to that kind of encounter is an analogical imagination. All good interpreters possess it. For the phrase "an analogical imagination"[30] simply reminds us that conversation occurs if, and only if, we will risk ourselves by allowing the questions of the text. We must follow those questions—however initially different, other, or even strange—until the unique result of this kind of interaction occurs: the exploration of possibility as possible and thus as similarity-in-difference. In such moments of recognition, what is both disclosed and concealed as other and different becomes appropriated as possibility. When possibility enters, some similarity-in-difference cannot be far behind.[31] If we are careful, we do not claim that we have actualized the other as it was once actualized either by the author or by its original reception. Empathy is much too romantic a category to comprehend this necessary movement in interpretation from otherness, to possibility, to similarity-in-difference. Even the great exponents of romantic empathy, such as Schleiermacher, or the great practicioners of virtuosolike "divination," such as Rudolf Otto, are honored today not for their theories of interpretation but for the quality of their concrete interpretations. To follow Otto's interpretation of the phenomenon of the holy, for example, is to observe the interpretive process at work despite Otto's neo-Kantian descriptions of his procedures.[32] He starts with an interpretation of the holy as radically other, the holy as *mysterium tremendum*, and by means of that very interpretation of otherness, Otto recognizes at the same time the possibility of the holy as *fascinans*. Despite his neo-Kantian categories, Otto cannot, however, let go of his own interpretation as questioning. He interprets the awe-ful possibility of the holy as similar to, yet radically different from, other human possibilities, namely, moral, scientific, and aesthetic possibilities. To read Coleridge on the difference between fancy and imagination[33] is not necessarily to agree with his claims to the absolute creativity of imagination and the power of genius. It is, however, to learn to explore a possibility, the possibility of the world manifested in the work of the high romantic period.

Our own postromantic response is not likely to be one of identification with, or great empathy for, the romantic vision. A more wary, ironic, even suspicious response is probably the only one that a postmodernist sensibility can accord the claims for genius, creativity, symbol, and the imagination made by romantics.[34] Insofar as we understand Schleiermacher or Coleridge at all, we understand them differently from how they understood themselves. For we understand them as those who have been partly constituted by the history of ambiguous effects of their work. If we would converse with their texts, we also come to understand why otherness and difference rarely become sameness or even similarity. Otherness and difference can become, however, genuine possibility: the *as* other, the *as* different becomes the *as* possible. Thus we find ourselves discovering similarities-in-difference, that is, analogies, with the romantics. And all our present similarities-in-difference will in turn one day yield to yet other analogies for later readers.

When attempting to describe the generative or evocative power of any classic text, readers may be driven, as Heidegger was, to use the language of "disclosure-concealment."[35] Such language is designed to challenge claims to full comprehension, to certainty, and ultimately to mastery and control. Consider the example of art. The ancient discipline of Greek poetics was originally articulated on the model of the crafts. Now a model of disclosure-concealment better serves our understandings of the kind of claims to truth of the work of art.

To describe the power of the work of art or indeed any classic by using the language of disclosure and concealment suggests another new word for the response of the interpreter: recognition. However Platonic its resonances, re-cognition suggests the kind of response that any risk-taking interpreter is likely to find when experiencing a classic. This more complex description of conversation as exploration of possibility yields a new model of interaction: disclosure-concealment is the major characteristic of the power of the text's claim to our attention, while recognition is the major characteristic of the experience of the interpreter. On this model, therefore, no response can be predicted in advance. Rather, concrete responses can range across a whole spectrum.[36]

Our response, for example, may take the form of some shock of recognition. Then we may identify with the world of the text. Sometimes, we even experience a sense of terror in the face of the radical otherness of that world.[37] Still further along the spectrum we may discover only some tentative resonance with, or even distance from, the world that the text has opened up for our recognition.[38] The skills used in every act of interpretation are analogous to those used in moments of phronesis or practical wisdom that teach us how to act in a concrete situation.[39] No more than in the case of phronesis can the skills needed for interpretation be rendered fully explicit. We can, however, attempt a generic and heuristic description like that above to remind us of what interpretation involves.

For relative adequacy is just that: relative, not absolute, adequacy. If one demands certainty, one is assured of failure. We can never possess absolute certainty.[40] But we can achieve a good—that is, a relatively adequate—interpretation: relative to the power of disclosure and concealment of the text, relative to the skills and attentiveness of the interpreter, relative to the kind of conversation possible for the interpreter in a particular culture at a particular time. Somehow conversation and relatively adequate interpretations suffice. As Hilary Putnam reminds us: in some situations, "Enough is enough, enough is not everything."[41] Sometimes less is more.

And yet, as each of us knows from any experience of conversation, we often do not content ourselves with the kind of inquiry described above. As the other conversation partner, whether it be person or text, challenges our expectations, questions, and interpretations, we can also find ourselves in a radical conflict of interpretations. This conflict can even be internal.

We may so believe in our own intentions that we become deaf to other voices. Persons willing to converse are always at one major disadvantage from those who are not. The former always consider the possibility that they may be wrong. As any of us become more conscious of other interpretations, we become more aware of the occasional need to interrupt the conversation. Argument may be necessary. Argument is not synonymous with conversation. We do not generally find it necessary to use argument in order to recognize the possibilities in either a classic text or a work of art. That happens through the openness of conversation.[42] Nevertheless conflicts emerge, positions harden, differences in interpretations increase. To demand argument is not to disavow the intuitive skills necessary for conversation. To demand argument is not necessarily to think that we can find truth only through argument. Argument has little part to play in experiencing Mozart. Does that mean there is no truth in *Don Giovanni?* Can we never read Plato's *Symposium* to explore the truth of Eros? Or must we observe only the arguments within the dialogue? Argument, on this reading, is not a replacement for exploratory conversation. Rather, argument is a vital moment within conversation that occasionally is needed if the conversation itself is to move forward.[43]

Sometimes, for example, when we read those classic conversations, the Platonic dialogues, we find Socrates and his conversation partners exploring possibilities simply by following the logic of the question wherever it leads. At other times we find Socrates or Gorgias or Phaedrus or even occasionally Thrasymachus finding it necessary to argue his case. In the most successful Platonic dialogues, the arguments are always part of a larger conversation. The Socratic enlightenment is real, but its optimistic reliance on dialectical argument is sometimes an unexamined premise of the examined life.[44] Another example: to tear the arguments of Philo, Cleanthes, and Demeter out of the narrative structure of Hume's *Dialogues* is to miss how the dialogue functions as an inquiry into truth.[45] Then the reader also misses not only the context but also the thrust of the individual arguments in the dialogue as a whole. This is not to say, of course, that the arguments in Hume's *Dialogues* are not real arguments. But these arguments are not there to function as quarries for modern anthologists. Even Anselm's famous so-called ontological argument should be interpreted within the larger dialogical structure of his whole inquiry.[46]

Arguments can, of course, be one form of conversation that lives on its own. But in the great dialogues, as in some of the best experiences of genuine inquiry in one's own life, arguments function best when they are part of a whole. Unfortunately we do not possess the dialogues of Aristotle. Fortunately we do possess many of Aristotle's arguments, including his studies of argument itself. How illuminating it would be to compare those arguments and studies of argument with the lost dialogues of our greatest master of argument! When Plato invented the dialogue form, perhaps to refute the poets by discovering a poetic genre of his own, he also created a place for dialectical argument within every dialogue—an important place, but not the only place. Plato did not fear narrative or—as in the *Timaeus*—even myth, with its power to provoke a manifestation of the essential. For all his fear of the poets, Plato accorded recognition a singular importance in all inquiry. Even in those dialogues (such as *Theatetus*, where argument plays the major role), Plato, unlike many Platonists, knew that conversation should be the encompassing reality within which all good arguments find their being. Arguments belong within conversation and not vice versa.

In any inquiry, argument is often needed. Even modern poetics needs dialectics and rhetoric if it is not to prove impressionistic. Dialectics and rhetoric, in turn, need ethics and politics at some point to complete the larger inquiry. Nor are metaphysical arguments beside the point. In modern terms, for example, de facto transcendental arguments on the conditions of possibility of conversation and argument itself are surely helpful.[47]

There are some inquirers like Max Scheler whose intuitive powers were startling.[48] But as the curious twists of Scheler's lifelong inquiry demonstrate, even his powerful intuitive sense could not suffice. Shifting intuitive claims do not aid the reader to decide among them. The opposite problem can also occur. Any belief that formal argument alone can suffice claims far too much. Formal analysis is important for testing all claims to validity and logical consistency. Yet formal arguments alone do not exhaust the range of inquiry any more than positivist notions of rationality exhaust the range of reason.[49] The once innocent dream of Descartes for indubitable truth has become a nightmare of competing methods to attain formal mastery and control. But neither the clear and distinct truths of Descartes's successors nor the profound intuitions of his rivals can limit inquiry to either pure intuition or formal argument.

Arguments, at their best, are moments within the wider conversation. Both topical and formal arguments are needed to adjudicate the counterclaims emerging in the wider conversation. Topical arguments analyze all substantive claims. Formal arguments analyze all claims to consistency. Both are helpful whenever conflicts of interpretation emerge. And conflicts do emerge.

When challenged on an interpretation, do I have any evidence that my conversation partner could accept? Can we find those commonplaces (*topoi*) that constitute the right places for discussing our differences? Can we find commonplaces on what constitutes argument itself? Or shall I simply retreat into announcements arising from my intuitive sense? I may be right, but no one else, in principle, will ever know it. I have become the Delphic oracle. I am reduced to solipsism, which is the enemy of conversation.

To give an interpretation is to make a claim. To make a claim is to be willing to defend that claim if challenged by others or by the further process of questioning itself.[50] When there are no further relevant questions either from the text or from myself or from the interaction that is questioning, then I find relative adequacy. I then present my interpretation to the community of inquiry to see if they have further relevant questions. They often will. Besides the more usual topical and formal arguments, there are also transcendental or, more modestly, quasi-transcendental arguments on argument itself as in Habermas and Apel. These arguments are, in my judgment, good arguments about certain necessary conditions for all communication.

It is, after all, reasonable to recall that all argument assumes the following conditions: respect for the sincerity of the other; that all conversation partners are, in principle, equals; saying what one means and meaning what one says; a willingness to weigh all relevant evidence, including one's warrants and backings; a willingness to abide by the rules of validity, coherence, and especially possible contradictions between my theories and my actual performance.

Argument on ideal-speech conditions illuminates, as its proponents correctly insist, a "counterfactual" situation.[51] The claim is not the claim that ideal speech actually exists. The claim is that this is what ideal speech would be if it ever existed. As ideal, and thereby counterfactual, this regulative model is useful for sorting out the ambiguities of all actual communication. We never find ourselves in the ideal speech situation. Even Socrates, for example, in the *Gorgias*, argues against rhetoric with arguments that show that he himself, as Nietzsche saw, was at times the wiliest rhetorician of them all. Surprisingly enough, in some contemporary academic discussions of ideal-speech conditions, the subtle relationships of truth and power[52] are ignored when they are allowed to function only unconsciously, as when a professor employs the full rights and responsibilities of "professorhood" in the seminar's inquiry on the need for the equality of all conversation partners. What constitutes disciplined inquiry in all the disciplines is not an innocent exercise of reason alone, as Toulmin's insistence on the historical conditions for the emergence of new disciplines argues, and as Foucault's analysis of the subtle relationships of power and knowledge in all these historical disciplines demonstrates.[53] Nevertheless, if I claim that an interpretation of a classic text is systemically distorted (e.g., anti-Semitic interpretations of the Gospel of John), then this implies that I already have some notion of what would constitute undistorted communication.[54] Reflection on "ideal-speech" conditions is, therefore, valuable.

Moreover, arguments on ideal-speech conditions are transcendental in the sense that they claim to provide the necessary conditions for a contingent situation, namely, the implicit claim to validity in all communication.[55] This is a claim to contingent, not absolute, necessity. By contrast, transcendental arguments on the existence or nonexistence of the universe or God are strictly transcendental arguments.[56] Communication could be other than it is, but in fact is not. We reason discursively. We inquire. We converse. We argue. We are human beings, not angels. In medieval arguments, angels were understood as created beings more powerful than humans but not divine. They lacked bodies and thereby sense knowledge, yet they functioned with extraordinary intuitive intellectual powers. Their intellects sound oddly like Descartes's model of human knowing. Angels, therefore, have some other way of knowing than our pedestrian, discursive way. Angels need only intuit to know. And each does so alone, not in a community of inquiry, for each exhausts its own species! But we humans must reason discursively, inquire communally, converse and argue with ourselves and one another. Human knowledge could be other than it is. But this is the way it is: embodied, communal, finite, discursive. Transcendental arguments on argument can play a limited but real role in analyzing certain necessary conditions for the contingent reality of human discursive communication.

William James once spoke of "on the whole-ness." It is a felicitous phrase. On the whole, we can now say, we need to use not only formal arguments but also topical, both rhetorical and dialectical, arguments. On the whole, transcendental arguments on argument are useful to keep in mind, especially when the going gets tough. Yet no transcendental argument can replace the need to allow for the flexibility of particular topical arguments on any particular question. Nor can even topical arguments replace the greater fluidity of conversation.[57]

What are we doing when we try to make more determinate some relatively indeterminate matter, such as conversation? What are we doing when we consider some reality that could be other than it presently is, such as interpreting interpretation itself? What are we doing when we attempt to defend any claim to relative adequacy for a particular interpretation of a classic text? We converse, and when appropriate, we argue. We may even converse about conversation and argue over argument. What we should do is whatever the questioning of the moment demands. That is surely not everything. Is it enough? Only further questioning can tell.

CHAPTER 2

Argument: Method, Explanation, Theory

We have seen that interpretation, on the model of conversation, is a complex phenomenon comprised of three elements: text, interpreter, and their interaction grounded in questioning itself. That complexity increases when we allow conversation to hold primacy without forfeiting the need for argument. Nor is the demand for truth ignored in the model of interpretation. Conversation accords primacy to one largely forgotten notion of truth: truth as manifestation.[1]

Truth manifests itself, and we recognize its rightness. More technically stated, truth is here understood, on the side of the object, as the power of disclosure and concealment in the object itself; and that disclosure is related to truth as an experience of recognition on the side of the subject. There is, in every true manifestation, an intrinsic, that is dialogical, interaction between the object's disclosure and concealment and the subject's recognition. That interaction is conversation.

Any conversation with a classic is always interactive. Once the result of that conversation is communicated to others, it enters yet another dialogue, in principle, with the whole community of competent readers. The discovery of truth as manifestation is the first fruit of any dialogical life. Without genuine conversation, no manifestation. Without manifestation, no real dialogue. It is by conversation alone that we are freed from epistemological solipsism for a dialogical life, with others and with all the classics. Dialogue is both a mode of human life and a manifestation of the dialogical reality of all human life. We belong to history and language; they do not belong to us. If we would belong to them well, we must question them and question ourselves through them. Through that questioning we participate in the conversation of all humankind, living and dead. Through that conversation, we experience those truths made manifest by our willingness to dialogue and by the classics' power to disclose. That power manifests itself to every true conversation partner. Anyone who has experienced even one such moment—in watching a film, in listening to music, in looking at a painting, in participating in a religious ritual, in reading a classic text, in conversation with friends, or in finding oneself in love—knows that truth as manifestation is real. And it does suffice. Without such a truth, life is indeed nasty, brutish, and short. Without manifestation, thought is too thin. Truth, in its primordial sense, is manifestation.[2]

When interpreters claim to recognize any manifestation, they also implicitly claim a relative adequacy for that interpretation.[3] Others may or may not agree. At that point argument can enter anew. Arguments are by definition intersubjective and communal. As the demands of argument become explicit, the implicitly intersubjective nature of all truth as manifestation can also become an explicit claim to an argued consensus of warranted beliefs for a particular community of inquiry.[4] Then models of truth as correspondence are acknowledged not as primary but as important, once understood as the consensual truth of warranted beliefs.[5] At the same time, the role of models of truth as coherence reemerges: coherence can mean, first, the rough coherence implied in all manifestations and appropriate to all symbol systems, culture, languages, history, and life itself. Recall, for example, Aristotle in the *Poetics* on the role of plots, or modern appeals to how narrative or story provides the rough coherence proper to experience itself.[6] Or coherence can also mean not strictly truth but validity, that coherence appropriate to all purely formal arguments.

In this move from a model of truth as primordial manifestation to truth as warranted consensus and truth as coherence, there is a danger that the primary importance of manifestation (more fully disclosure-concealment-recognition) can be lost as the demands of argument take over. The founding visions and intuitions of many great thinkers have sometimes yielded to a narrow scholasticism. Recall the move from Plato to many Platonists, from Thomas Aquinas to many Thomists, from Kant to many neo-Kantians, or even from Hegel of the *Phenomenology* to Hegel of the *Logic*. Such moves, of course, can involve a deepening of the original insight provided by the technical developments of later arguments.[7] But at other times the original insight is buried under a cenotaph of dazzling technical virtuosity and unacknowledged sterility. For example, the history of effects of the Cartesian model of achieving certainty by means of clear and distinct ideas—and very few of them—can alert one to this problem. The modern reduction of rhetorical arguments to "mere rhetoric," as Vico saw, highlights this same difficulty. So does the present struggle across the disciplines against scientism with its strange dialectic: reduce all conversation to argument, reduce all topical arguments to formal arguments, deny any truth status to manifestation by replacing all classical claims to truth with modern formal claims to validity.[8]

And yet there are resources for resisting this formalist dialectic: new understandings of truth as the interplay of disclosure-concealment-recognition, as in the great tragedies against which Plato fought; the recovery of conversation as a way to truth, as in Plato's discovery of the dialogue form itself; the reinstatement of topical or substantive arguments in both rhetorical and dialectical forms; a clearer sense of the relative, never absolute, adequacy of all metaphysical and transcendental arguments.[9] And these new resources for understanding truth need not occasion a reinstatement of romantic prejudices. To grant a primary role to symbol in all discourse, for example, is not necessarily to disparage the need for concepts. To rediscover that metaphors and metonyms are present in all systems of conceptual thought is not to disparage efforts at second-order thought.[10] We enrich all thought by the use of concepts faithful to the originating symbols, metaphors, and metonyms. We often need the second-order language of concepts in order to understand first-order discourse itself. Since every claim to true manifestation is also a claim to publicness, we shall often need to interpret further the claims resulting from conversation. We shall also often need those refined forms of argument—theories, methods, and explanations—to test further our best insights and all our claims that we have indeed recognized some manifestation of truth.

To grasp the full extent of our present intellectual dilemma, we must first abandon some influential interpretations on what our options are. Both the Enlightenment and the romantic movement are classic events in Western culture. Like all classic events, both have proved to be ambiguous. The Enlightenment both freed us from the weight of certain oppressive traditions and taught us, as Kant insisted, that we must dare to think for ourselves.[11] But as the dialectic of the Enlightenment unfolded, it became trapped in ever narrower models of what could count as truth and what could count as free action, namely, purely autonomous action. The once emancipatory concepts of the Enlightenment, as Adorno suggested, became mere categories. Reason retreated into a formal and technical rationality.[12] Meanwhile, the social engineers competed with conflicting visions of a future rational society. Others waited in Zurich for a sealed train to the Finland station.

To understand the dialectic of the Enlightenment does not necessarily mean a return to romanticism. For the romantic movement bears its own history of ambiguous effects. We are all heirs to this movement insofar as we accord some primacy to truth as manifestation and insofar as we acknowledge the presence of tradition in all our thought, including scientific thought. But we are always in danger of becoming merely the latest expressions of the "unhappy consciousness" of the romantic. Our response cannot be a remystification of all reality. It cannot be a pretense that the imagined joys of first naïveté can be ours. It cannot be the disparagement of science and the retreat into privacy. Pure privacy is as illusory as it is dangerous, as the Weimar intellectuals discovered too late when faced with that demonic caricature of Wagnerian romanticism, the remythologizing, anti-Enlightenment Nazis.[13]

Scientism has pretensions to a mode of inquiry that tries to deny its own hermeneutic character and mask its own historicity so that it might claim ahistorical certainty. The effects of all scientistic models remain powerful, even pervasive, forces in the culture at large despite the intellectual bankruptcy of its reigning ideology. Consider the radical privatization of all claims to truth in art, religion, ethics, and historical actions. Consider the modern scientistic narrowing of the classical notions of reason. Consider how pluralism can collapse into a repressive tolerance.

Consider how rapidly the totalization of some useful techniques like behaviorism can become an attack on all demands for critical reflection. Consider the technicization of a once-public realm.[14]

Nor can romanticism in its many forms save the day. Popular culture, as found in the mass media, especially television, is capable of an occasional outburst of pathos disguised as social significance. But a tragic vision seems usually beyond it. Fortunately, satire and black humor can occasionally surface. Or consider modern, halfhearted romantic appeals to genius become its caricature, the contemporary celebrity. Or notice appeals to some current models of psychology that promise maturity through therapeutic techniques that seem simply to reinforce the status quo.[15] How these techniques relate to Freud's terrifying discovery of the unconscious is a puzzle. Indeed, as puzzling as the relationship between those forms of modern Christianity described by E. M. Forster as "poor, chatty, little Christianity" and the frightening parables of Jesus of Nazareth. When even Freud or Jesus can be treated in the romantic fashion first as geniuses, then as social reformers, we know we are not far from the higher reaches of uplift. We may even begin to sense ourselves at the end of the romantic tether.

We may now turn to a fuller examination of some of the limitations of the model of conversation. These difficulties can be described as various interruptions of our original model: interruptions by method, theory, and explanation. In the following chapters we shall analyze those radical interruptions called plurality and ambiguity. Hope for conversation can decrease as these interruptions increase. Whether we should abandon that hope is a real question, one usefully posed, however, only after we have studied all these challenges.

Certain kinds of arguments have achieved great success, on the whole, arguments warranted by some method. That method is ordinarily backed by some explanatory theory. So great has been the success of method that almost every mode of disciplined inquiry has tried at one time or another to put an end to the conflict of interpretations by means of some explanatory method. From the strife occasioned by Dilthey's attempt to develop a theory accounting for a sharp division between *Natürwissenschaften* and the *Geisteswissenschaften*, through Max Weber's search for a value-free social scientific method, to Talcott Parson's's stabilizing theory for a stable society, to Roman Jakobson's theory of poetics, the same scenario unfolds.[16] That scenario is this: Method, explanation, and theory, modeled largely on their presumed nature and success in the natural sciences, must be developed in every discipline.

And yet as the reign of method took over all the disciplines, a paradox emerged: the natural sciences themselves began to enter a postpositivist stage. The examples are by now familiar: quantum theory, the discovery of such uncannily Joycean phenomena as quarks, the acknowledgment of the role of the scientific interpreter in all experiment, the realization that all data are theory-laden. More recently, less familiar examples have also been observed: the role of imagination, metaphor, and metonymy in scientific inquiry itself;[17] the insistence among postpositivist philosophers of science on the historical context of all scientific paradigms (Kuhn) and the topical, and thereby historical, character of all scientific arguments (Toulmin). In all these developments, former scientistic claims to ahistorical certainty and nonhermeneutical insights have collapsed. Science has become again both historical and hermeneutical.

The undeniable achievements of science remain. But the object of its once-mastering inquiry is now understood by many scientists as "not only stranger than we imagine but stranger than we can possibly imagine." A sense of wonder, even mystery, was once considered the skeleton in the family closet of the humanities. But now that wonder has surfaced in the natural sciences themselves. Astronomy, environmental science, and the new physics are, after all, no less rigorous, methodical, theoretical, and explanatory—in a word scientific—than their predecessors. Former claims for a value-free technology and a history-free science have collapsed. The hermeneutical character of science has now been strongly affirmed. Even in science, we must interpret in order to understand.

In the meantime, the humanities and the social sciences have become more reluctant to model themselves on the mechanistic models of an earlier natural science.[18] They no longer consider their explicitly hermeneutical character a liability. The rediscovery of hermeneutics has occasioned a fresh rethinking of the tropes involved in all discourse: in both scientific history and the social sciences; above all, in the humanities, as the reemergence of rhetoric demonstrates. In this intellectual situation the humanist's new temptation is unlikely to be scientism. It could become, however, one more round of romanticism. But before any of us become too enthusiastic about the retrieval of symbol, metaphor, and narrative, we should be aware that all these hermeneutical studies are also open to methodical, explanatory, and theoretical study.

Even Hans-Georg Gadamer can become so wary of the dangers of methodologism that he sometimes fears all method and all distancing through theory and explanation.[19] And yet, as Paul Ricoeur has argued, distance is not necessarily a sign of alienation. In my own terms, abstraction is also an enriching phenomenon, and the move to concept and theory is often necessary to understand certain essential characteristics of any phenomenon. The occasional interruption of conversation by argument, as we saw above, demands a temporary distancing from the more free-flowing movement of conversation. That interruption is often necessary for the conversation itself. Even those who like myself accord primacy to participatory notions of understanding need not retreat to a polemical stance on the occasional practical necessity for distance. Rather we can acknowledge that all good methods, explanations, and theories inevitably distance us from our primal sense of participation.[20]

Understanding should encompass all interpretations. But explanation, method, and theory can develop, correct, and challenge any initial understandings. As the verb *develop* suggests, a method can clarify our initial understanding by making it firmer and more refined and thereby available to the wider community of inquiry. At other times a particular method or theory can correct or challenge our first understanding.[21] Historical critical methods have corrected all anachronistic interpretations of the classics. Literary critical methods have challenged all literalist readings of texts, including philosophical and scientific texts. Semiotic and structuralist methods have uncovered the codes present in all texts. Social scientific methods have demystified certain humanist categories, including the category of the Great Tradition.

Aristotle's genius for analyzing the nature and limits of various modes of inquiry clarified and expanded the nature and range of classical reason. There are, to be sure, real differences between the disciplines envisaged and the methods analyzed by Aristotle and contemporary historically conscious disciplines and methods. Yet these differences need not deny the gains of modern methods. These differences also need not become the occasion to write one more Whig history on the triumph of the final scientific method or the ultimate explanatory theory. Classical understandings of reason or classical modes of inquiry like Aristotle's poetics, rhetoric, dialectic, and metaphysics remain resources for any reflective mind. We can see all these possibilities best, however, not only by further general discussion on method, theory, or explanation but by analysis of two major contemporary methods: historical critical methods and literary critical methods.[22] Both methods are central to any contemporary discussion of interpretation. Both methods are crucial to the debates on the role of explanation and theory in all interpretation. Both show the same needs: an affirmation of method with a rejection of methodologism, the role of explanation in understanding, the relationship of theory and practice.

No method or collection of methods has had a more powerful effect upon Western interpretations of all traditions than historical critical methods. Indeed, my own earlier interpretations both of the text, and its history of effects, and of the interpreter, and his or her historicity, can be read as one more footnote to the modern revolution of Western historical consciousness. One effect of that revolution has been to challenge any easy participation in a tradition. For example, Hans Frei has shown how traditional Christian readings of the Scriptures as "history-like" narratives have been interrupted by modern historical critical readings.[23] The ever-new quests for the historical Jesus have affected all readings of the gospel texts.[24] Analogous quests for the historical Homer, the historical Socrates, even the historical Buddha, are further evidence of the persuasive power of the modern historical sensibility: an implacable insistence that all our narratives should prove historically plausible.

No one can doubt that the use of historical critical methods has become a central demand in our historically conscious culture. In one sense, we have all become lawyers constantly using such qualifier words as "allegedly," "supposedly," or, "it was then believed" whenever we interpret our historical narratives. The intellectual revolution of historical consciousness has had wide-ranging effects upon modern Western thought. The acknowledgment of the historical character of all our classics can surely allow us a more informed understanding. For all of us except dogmatists and fundamentalists, both religious and secular, the historical exposure of the ambiguities of our traditions has occasioned critical reflection. Such reflection provides distance from all that simply "is." Historical critical methods show us how what "is" came to be. All historical and social practices that seemed so natural are now understood for what they are: not expressions of nature but expressions of history. Some recent rhetorical analyses of the tropes employed in the writing of history suggest, in effect, that history and fiction are interchangeable genres.[25] Those analyses have value. But it still matters to us to know what actually happened in history with whatever degree of historical certitude is possible.

It is ethically obscene to state that it does not matter if the Holocaust happened or not. It did matter when the smoking gun appeared in the Watergate tapes. These are not beliefs, much less fictions, but established, historical facts. It does matter to know whether Churchill ordered the death of Sikorski or why Truman decided to use the atomic bomb. Such facts matter; however painful, they free us from illusions. They demand ethical response because their statement as fact is an exercise in ethical responsibility.[26] It is morally irresponsible not to care what occasioned what, what actually happened, and what consequences ensued in all the classic events that formed our culture, such as the English, American, French, and Russian revolutions. It is irresponsible, for example, for Christians not to care if Jesus ever lived at all and then go on to state their firm belief in Jesus of Nazareth as the Christ.

It is true that the historical memory of a people is the principal carrier of the history of effects of the classic texts, persons, events, symbols, rituals of that people. It is also true that a loss of those memories, in either an individual or a communal sense, can be fatal to participation in a culture.[27] For without them we cannot act. To become socialized by learning one's native language is to give life to all those carriers of meaning and action that are a tradition. "The past," as William Faulkner insisted, "is not dead, it is not even past."

At the same time, there is no such thing as an unambiguous

tradition; there are no innocent readings of the classics. We are who we are because of the traditions that form us. Our lives are shaped by the preconscious effects of all the traditions whose narratives and ways of envisioning the world have forged our memories and consequently our actions.

We also know that sometimes it is important to distance ourselves from the past, even to forget, in order to go on at all. An inability to forget, to let go of painful memories and of the desire for vengeance, can so poison an individual or a culture that it is no longer possible to understand humanly. There are times to forget as surely as there are times to remember. To discern the difference demands powers of critical reflection as well as that courage that informs any historical consciousness. We forget too easily how courageous an effort of distancing lies in the word *ecumenical*. Modern ecumenical Catholics and Protestants need only turn to the snares of conflicting versions of history in Northern Ireland to recognize the courage of those many ecumenical Christians in modern Ireland who have learned not only to remember but also to forget.

Historians employ a number of skills in order to deal with various kinds of evidence that come within the compass of their task. In one sense, the nature of historical argument seems obvious: to examine the relevant data and reach sound conclusions to whatever degree of historical probability the evidence will allow. That evidence is warranted by a use of the established norms of historical critical methods. To state the matter in this brief form, however, is to give the barest outline of the kinds of practical and theoretical skills needed in all historical work. One who doubts this might try writing a historical article on the relationship between the art of Jacques Louis David and the French Revolution and the Napoleonic era.

Skilled historians may be able to work with a relatively small amount of data to reach sound historical conclusions. Recall what little data, for example, Hugh Trevor-Roper possessed when sent by the British government at the end of World War II to determine whether Hitler had died in Berlin.[28] The Soviets had taken most of the crucial evidence with them and were in no mind to share it with the British. To read Trevor-Roper's *The Last Days of Hitler* is to watch the detectivelike skills of the expert historian at work. Indeed, to read Trevor-Roper's book even

today is to find remarkable how well most of his conclusions—
except for the manner of Hitler's death—held up years later,
after the Soviets finally released their evidence. And yet, even
the most skilled historian can occasionally be led astray, as was
Trevor-Roper in his recent initial willingness to authenticate the
"Hitler diaries."

No outline can account adequately for the many skills needed
to produce a single good historical interpretation. So rare are
these skills that consensus among historians is often difficult.
The community of historians can agree on some conclusions that
approach certitude, for example, that Jesus of Nazareth and Socrates actually lived. At other times, particularly when they are
interpreting historically established facts, the consensus is far
more tentative. For example, it is relatively easy to agree upon
the basic outline of the message of Jesus or that of Socrates but
very difficult, if not impossible, to elucidate their self-understanding, or indeed that of any other historical figure.[29]

Historical methods may develop and refine one's initial understanding. Recent historical research on Montesquieu and
Rousseau has developed earlier historical interpretations of the
ideologies to be found in the programs of such leaders of the
French Revolution as Mirabeau, Danton, and Robespierre. New
historical methods may also correct or even challenge prior understandings of some classic text or event. Recent historical
scholarship, for example, has discovered the economic interests
at stake in the conflicting programs for either reform (Mirabeau)
or revolution (Robespierre). Such analysis by economic historians challenges and elaborates earlier interpretations of the influence of Rousseau and Montesquieu as outlined by intellectual
historians.[30]

As in all arguments, if any historical critical warrant becomes
questionable, and no adequate backing can be found to defend
it, then its use can no longer serve for historical judgment. The
debates on the logic of historical judgment, on the nature of
narrativity in historical writing, on the use of tropes in even the
most scientific historical discourse, or the analyses of the puzzling combinations of power and knowledge in any historical
period, are basically conflicts not over particular conclusions but
over procedures for warranting any historical conclusion.[31] As
these historical arguments increase—as they are likely to do—

historical assessments will take new and unexpected turns. If, for example, the recent interest in the rhetorical use of tropes (metaphor, metonymy, synecdoche, irony) in all historical writing assumes the status of the principal warrant for understanding historical critical method, then present historical judgments will seem far more insecure. If, however, as I consider more plausible, the rediscovery of the use of tropes in historical writing fruitfully complicates but does not replace the topical character of all historical argument, then historical interpretations will be more rhetorically nuanced but no less probable.[32]

When all historical work completes its judgments of historical probability, we do not end but begin anew our proper task of understanding by interpreting. For interpreters, now historically informed, must return again to the task of understanding by conversing with the claim to attention of classic texts and events. No amount of historical reconstruction can spare us that further effort. If all classic claims to attention are not to become historical period pieces, then history, as the Adolf von Harnack insisted, must have the first but not the last word in all interpretation. That word belongs to the effort to understand by the risk of new interpretations of the questions that our now historically reconstructed texts and events provoke. That word, as Jacob Burckhardt knew, belongs to those new moments of memory, distance, forgetfulness, and hope that our historically reconstructed texts evoke.

A usable past is a retrievable past. As many historians have insisted, historical scholarship is at the service of the wider conversation of our common humanity. Furthermore, the historicity of every text, interpreter, and conversation has been clarified by historical consciousness. Certainty is no more. But relative adequacy for all interpretations remains an ideal worth striving for. The historical disciplines, like the humanities and social sciences, are intrinsically hermeneutical disciplines. Changes in hermeneutical understanding eventually affect the warranting procedures, the methods, and the explanatory theories of all the disciplines.

These changes can lead to a free-for-all where chaos rules and all methods, theories, and explanations become suspect of scientism. Then we may encounter a radical rhetoricization of historical work, paeans to anti-method in science itself, explosions of new antiromantic romantic outbursts in the culture at large, and, most desperately, new claims for purely autonomous texts or interpreters. In the meantime, working scientists, social scientists, historians, and humanists will continue their constitutively interpretive tasks. They will also be aware that even without these new reflections (including hermeneutical theory!) the traditional interpretive skills work. *Eppur si muove.*

The rediscovery of the hermeneutical character of all the disciplines has also led to a rediscovery across the disciplines of literary criticism and literary theory.[33] In one sense, this turn to literary theory was inevitable, since hermeneutics itself is an insistence upon the linguistic character of all understanding. Literary critics, more than any other scholars, have developed refined methods for dealing with linguistic problems at their most acute—in those complex works we call literature. In another sense, this turn to literary criticism also follows the rediscovery of rhetoric: both the rhetoric of the topics, and topical arguments, and the rhetoric of the tropes, particularly the persistence of tropes in even the most theoretical discourse.

As befits a discipline whose controversies unexpectedly turn out to be at the heart of the matter for several other disciplines, the disputes in literary criticism and literary theory are fierce. They do not as yet yield any widely agreed upon results. Earlier biographical criticism of authors, as well as more sophisticated recent defenses of the author's intention as the key to the meaning of texts, have proved as unstable as the instabilities they originally struggled against.[34] The New Criticism of the forties and fifties, with its autonomous texts, its verbal icons, and its well-wrought urns, has found its models of autonomy shattered by the interplay of text and reader in modern hermeneutics. Similar hermeneutical insights have been developed by reception critics in Europe (H.-R. Jauss) and reader-response critics in North America.[35] Traditional humanist readings of the central role of "characters" in narratives have yielded to more explicitly ethical-political interpretations of the ideologies inevitably embedded in all texts, readings, and readers.[36] A merely impressionistic criticism, the real target of the famous "affective fallacy," is always a danger. But whenever we acknowledge the complexity of the interactions between any text and any reader, we must enter into the embattled domain of contemporary literary criticism and literary theory. Just as surely, literary critics now acknowledge the concerns and methods of other disciplines in their own work on other than "extrinsic" grounds.

Indeed it is remarkable how much theory now enters the practice of many literary critics.[37] Like historians, literary critics are most dependent on their skill in interpreting particular texts. In that sense, T. S. Eliot was correct to insist that intelligence is the surest method. We can never fully explicate, much less legislate, methods to guarantee the presence of those acts of discernment and attitudes of critical receptivity that the great critics instinctively employ.

At their best—Doctor Johnson, Sainte-Beuve, Henry James—the great critics are the best exemplars of that civilized conversation that explores and critically retrieves classics. At their best, all literary critics are willing to abandon their favorite theories when a conversation with the actual text demands it. For good critics, like good historians, know—sometimes explicitly, more often instinctively—that the point is always to risk a conversation with the claims to attention of great texts. The fact that literary critics are probably the most natural practitioners of the subtle art of conversation as the exploration of possibilities may account for some of their former resistance to theory. Insofar as critics continue to produce good readings of the great texts, the loss is not so great. But insofar as literary critics fail to realize that theories, and their attendant ideologies, will function whether we will it or not, their reluctance will be our loss.

No less than in the other disciplines, the conversation of literary critics also needs the occasional interruption of argument, theory, explanation, and method. Here, too, understanding must encompass the entire process of interpretation, but explanations, theories, and methods can also be important. The older distinctions between extrinsic and intrinsic criticism have collapsed. Traditional humanist self-understanding can become smug. The defenders of the Great Tradition need to reflect further on their possible complicity in a status quo they think they have rejected.

In every interpretation, some theory, however inchoate, is present. Every text presents us at least with the problem of how to relate the parts and the whole. For example, a single sentence may be the most illuminating clue to the whole text. That part may exemplify how a text may constitute an organic whole, but it must be tested throughout the whole text. Alternatively, a seeming digression in the text (the famous "man in the mackintosh" in Joyce's *Ulysses*, the naked young man in Mark's Gospel, the lost umbrella in Nietzsche, or the marginal asides in Rousseau)[38] can sometimes show how this text does not form a whole. That claim too must be tested. That claim may even need some explanatory theory, such as Derrida's complex but strangely stable theory on the radical instability of all texts.

If a particular word seems to be the key to the text, then we still need to study in detail how that word functions in the sentence, paragraph, chapter, and text as a whole. To concentrate only on words rather than on sentences is effectively to turn all texts into dictionaries—and Borges-like dictionaries at that. The route from the word to the sentence to the paragraph to the chapter to the text demands an explanation and perhaps an explanatory theory. We do not receive mere messages through texts. We receive coded messages whose code we must break if we are to understand the message itself with anything like relative adequacy. At the most basic level of reading competence, we all have to learn how to put together such basic elements as parts and wholes by learning grammar and composition. How grammar interacts with rhetoric and vice versa is an even more perplexing code to understand. And how full texts function as texts is an exceptionally complex problem, suggesting the need for a theory of the text itself.

We never encounter pure subject matter. We always encounter formed subject matters. The ways in which the subject matter is formed are many and varied: the grammatical codes of the language, the persuasive play of the tropes, the power of implicit or explicit topical arguments, the history of former readings of the text, the history of our own preunderstandings of the questions of the text and our expectations for this text, the kind of conversations available to us in our own culture. When we call certain texts literature, we need mean only that these texts have achieved a successful refiguration of reality—one where we know that we cannot separate form and content.

A traffic report or a weather report attempts to be, as much as possible, pure content, pure message. Yet even they are coded grammatically and rhetorically in order to work as messages. On the other hand, a poem attempts to be a text where form and content constitute an indissoluble whole, as in the Japanese haiku. In poetry, at least, we know we cannot extract some ready message from the formed subject matter of the words. Even if we have never heard of the "heresy of paraphrase," we know instinctively that we cannot, without loss, translate the meaning of a poem into a prosaic message. Whenever we struggle to interpret any great work, we experience the truth of that nice Italian play on words, *tradutore-tradditore*.

What we discover in these experiences is that all understanding is linguistic through and through. We also sense that language is a matter of codes—and indeed codes within codes—that are present in even our most highly individual usages. What we sense is that any neat separations of form and content no longer work for understanding, that is, interpreting, any written text or any oral discourse. There are no pure ideas free of the web of language. There are no pure messages. Whatever message comes, whatever subject matter is understood, comes by means of its form, whether the text is as short as a proverb or as long as an epic.

An example of the kind of explanation now available for reflecting on these issues is the recent debate on how the sense of a text (i.e., its internal coded structures and meanings) is related to the refigured reference of a text (i.e., its relationship to the world outside of the text—what it refers to).[39] As the examples of grammar and rhetoric already show, some notion of composition is implicit in all texts. To obey grammar is to acknowledge that the sense of the text is structured by the codes and rules of a particular langauge. To employ the tropes well, to find the right *topoi* or those places where arguments may be found, is to acknowledge that all texts attempt to be persuasive. To employ both grammar and rhetoric is to be involved in composition. We do not know a language if we know only a list of words or a list of grammatical rules. Rather we know a language, as Wittgenstein observed, only when we know "how to go on." A play consisting only of memorized phrases from a tourist's survival kit would quickly become a wonderful Ionesco farce. As any of us know, when we encounter another culture with a few survival phrases, all too soon we do not know how to go on at all. We stumble, we grunt, we point. But we do not—for we cannot—converse.

The difficulty of translation even between cognate languages is a good example of the hidden power of grammar, semantics, and rhetoric. Consider, for example, the difficulty of translating into English the first line of Proust's *A la recherche du temps perdu*: "Longtemps, je me suis couché de bonne heure."[40] The accepted English translation reads, "For a long time I used to go to bed early." Any reader of that great novel cannot but be disappointed by this translation. Grammarians will observe that we have no tense in English that is the exact equivalent of the French *passé composé*, a tense expressing an action that took place in the past but whose effects continue into the present. "I used to go to bed early" does not have the same meaning as "je me suis couché de bonne heure." Rhetoricians will remind us that, in French, the word *longtemps* suggests "for a long time" as well as the more resonantly mythic "a long time ago." Similarly, *bonne heure* also suggests *bonheur* (happiness). We cannot translate into English—at least with analogous resonance in only one sentence—all that Proust's wonderful first sentence suggests in French. In the same way, the French translation of Joyce's *Ulysses* cannot capture the full grammatical and rhetorical resources of Joyce's English without becoming, in effect, a new work. One despairs altogether of *Finnegans Wake*.

Even before anyone considers more complex problems like theories of genre, style, or text, the difficulties of composition suggest how content is always formed, how messages are always coded. Interpretation is never exact but, at its best, relatively adequate. We may know that this sentence of Proust begins his uncannily self-referential novel. We may know that this sentence is a typically Proustian sentence. All this provides, of course, clues for interpreting the sentence even in English translation. But these clues help only because we have some working knowledge of how to go on in matters of genre (this is a novel) and style (this is a novel by Proust). We are aware that our expectations for the genre of the novel may be challenged by Proust's refashioning of the code for novels. We bring some cultural expectations to the kind of style we anticipate in reading Proust: those labyrinthine, seductive, and deceptively stable sentences of Proust. We may even bring some knowledge of the narrative codes of the traditional French novel, some knowledge of the codes imitated by Proust, some knowledge of the historical personages who provided partial models for those refigurations that are the characters of the novel, even some knowledge of Proust's own remarkable character and life. All these preunderstandings set up expectations for our response to the first sentence of his novel. All of them inevitably influence our reading of it.

Eventually any reader of any great work will come to realize that genres are not merely taxonomic devices designed to help us locate a text ("This is a novel"). Genres are productive of meanings:[41] both the sense and the refigured referent of the text are produced through the genre. The fact that gospels are peculiar kinds of narratives, not theological essays, is not a merely rhetorical matter. Rather, the sense and the referent of the Gospels are produced by this unusual genre of gospel. The reason why proof-text criticism does not prove anything is clear: as criticism, it cannot account for either historical context or literary-linguistic codes (i.e., either grammar and rhetoric or composition, genre, and style). Genre criticism is helpful in placing texts in the usual historical critical way. But a knowledge of genre helps us understand the meaning of the text in a much more basic sense: namely, how both the sense and referent of the text are produced as refigured meanings through the genres themselves.

When we say Jane Austen or Federico Fellini or Bob Dylan, we refer only secondarily to the historical persons whose names we utter. We refer rather to a style, that is, to some individuating way of envisioning the world that is produced in the distinctive style of X. Style criticism is not an exercise in biographical criticism, valuable as the latter can be on its own by providing some clues to the secrets of an author's style. Criticism of style, rather, is a method, a theory, an explanation of how individual meanings are produced through peculiar strategies of stylistic refiguration.[42]

All these explanatory theories and methods of composition, genre, and style, in their turn, may eventually need the aid of some larger theory—like a theory of the text itself aligned with a theory of the productive imagination.[43] Any contemporary theory of the imagination cannot be based on earlier scientific interpretations of images as disposable substitutes for presently absent but readily available perceptions. An adequate theory of the imagination also needs to be rescued from the dismissal of the imaginative as merely fanciful, as happens in attacks on rhetorical language as a disposable ornament of scientific and literal discourse. A full theory of the text linked to a theory of the productive imagination does not yet exist in the fully explanatory form needed.[44] But whether or not a full theory of the imagination is ever developed, one thing is clear: Readers are able to use all the existing theories of composition, genre, and text along with some implicit theory of the productive imagination.

Explanation and understanding need not be enemies but may become wary allies. If theory is reified into some new final truth mechanically applied to all interpretations, the *entente cordiale* will be at an end. When methods are hardened into methodologisms, when explanations become replacements for the effort to understand, then even negotiations will cease. It will become again the war of all against all. All literary theory is at the service of the desire to understand individual literary works, just as surely as all argument is at the service of aiding the individual conversation. All theory worth having should ultimately serve the practice of reflective living.

Method, theory, and explanation can aid every conversation with every text, but none of them can replace the conversation itself. When we are conscious of what they are, we can use them well. Explanation and understanding, method and truth, theory and common sense, concept and symbol—all are partners in the complex discourse that is the dialogue of our day. Try to turn them against one another if you must, but they will find one another again when even one person begins a genuine conversation with any text.

CHAPTER 3

Radical Plurality: The Question of Language

There are many theories that attempt to explain the uneasy relationships among language, knowledge, and reality. For the moment, let us simply call this the "linguistic turn."[1] That turn has become an uncannily interruptive exploration of the radical plurality in language, knowledge, and reality alike.

In one sense, Nabokov caught best one major strand of postmodern reflection on language: " 'Reality' is the one word that should always appear within quotation marks." The collapse of both positivism and romanticism has created those quotation marks. The dream of positivism was to discover a reality without quotation marks: a realm of pure data and facts, red spots "out there" and sharp pains "in here." This realm—"science" it was named—gave us reality. Other realms—art, morality, religion, metaphysics, and common sense—gave us merely interpretations. But interpretations are not reality.

Yet every real spot out there needed naming, and every sharp pain in here needed language to understand it. The history of the collapse of the positivist ideal of a scientific realm freed from all interpretation is largely the history of two movements. The first was the increasing irrelevance of positivist descriptions in science itself. As postmodern science emerged, as noted above, it became clear that science was also a hermeneutic enterprise. Consider how hermeneutical science is: the role of the scientist in all theory formation and experimentation; the necessity of some linguistic formulation, even for those highly formal languages of mathematics and logic; the fact that "fact" means not an uninterpreted "already-out-there-now real" but a verified possibility; the acknowledgement that all data are theory-laden and all inquiry is interested. The result is clear: Positivism, the last intellectual stronghold against interpretation, could not hold. Despite its still undeniable power as a force in the culture as a whole, positivism as an intellectual interpretation of science is intellectually bankrupt. As Toulmin insists, postivism tried to deny what neither Newton nor Einstein, neither Planck nor Heisenberg ever denied: the fact that even science itself is interpretation.[2] Positivists were shocked where Newton would merely have been surprised by Wittgenstein's trenchant remark about Newtonian mechanics: "Thus it says nothing about the world except that it allows itself to be described, as indeed is the case."[3]

The alternative to understanding science as a hermeneutic enterprise is to understand it as the one enterprise freed from the complications of interpretation. But scientists and philosophers of science alike now acknowledge this positivist claim as one more interpretation of science, and one refuted by the actual practice and history of scientific inquiry. With science we interpret the world. We do not simply find it out there. Reality is what we name our best interpretation. Truth is the reality we know through our best interpretations. Reality is constituted, not created or simply found, through the interpretations that have earned the right to be called relatively adequate or true. In science, language inevitably influences our understanding of both data and facts, truth and reality.[4] Reality is neither out there nor in here. Reality is constituted by the interaction between a text, whether book or world, and a questioning interpreter. The interaction called questioning can produce warranted assertions through relevant evidence. The interaction in scientific inquiry elicits reflections on the more basic interaction of language and understanding in its warranted assertions.

We do not first experience or understand some reality and then find words to name that understanding. We understand in and through the languages available to us, including the historical languages of the sciences. By way of contrast, a fundamental belief was shared by the two otherwise radically conflicting options of modern intellectual life, positivism and romanticism. That belief was the secondary, even derivative, character of language in all understanding and knowing. For both the positivist and the romantic, language is an instrument we use. They believed language comes after the fact of discovery and cognition. The positivist uses language to articulate and communicate scientific results as facts rather than interpretations. The romantic uses language to express or represent some deep, nonlinguistic truth inside the self, especially the self of the romantic genius through whom the cosmos expresses itself.[5] As Lord Byron said, "The volcano must erupt to avoid the earthquake."

Language, in both the positivist and romantic readings, is instrumental. It is secondary, even peripheral, to the real thing. The real thing is purely prelinguistic: either my deep feelings or insights from within or my clear grasp of clear, distinct, scientific facts. What is lost in both these interpretations of language as instrument is not only the more subtle relationships of language, knowledge, and reality, but also the social and historical character of all understanding through language. If we think that understanding is free to use language as a mere instrument to express a deeper self, we are not far from the individualism of the romantic model. If we think that science is the one nonhermeneutical enterprise, we are not far from that unholy alliance of scientism, technologism, and possessive individualism that has created so much havoc in the public realm.

We understand in and through language. We do not invent our own private languages and then find a way to translate our communications to others. We find ourselves understanding in and through particular and public languages. No historical language is strictly necessary, but none is private, either. I think my best and worst thoughts, I understand my most intense pleasures and pains, I make my most considered and my most rash judgments, I reach my most responsible and my most irresponsible decisions in and through the languages available to me. These languages are social and historical: particular languages of pleasure and pain, of judiciousness and argument, of shame and honor, of responsibility and guilt.[6] I interpret my experience by understanding it through language. Artists—like Kafka with words, Rodin with bronze, and Duncan with dance—may render a new experience or help us name a felt but previously undefined experience. But to try to interpret language as a mere instrument of my creativity is to find myself in a cul-de-sac. Language is not an instrument that I can pick up and put down at will; it is always already there, surrounding and invading all I experience, understand, judge, decide, and act upon.[7] I belong to my language far more than it belongs to me, and through that language I find myself participating in this particular history and society.

To try to escape this reality either by romantic hyperbole or positivist fiat is to find oneself not freed from language, but trapped in two intellectually spent but culturally powerful languages, romantic expressivism and positivist scientism. The linguistic turn interrupts many traditional versions of both conversation and argument. Above all, in our period, that turn interrupts the reigning interpretations of both knowledge and reality.

Moreover, to challenge instrumentalist interpretations of language is not only to reintroduce society and history into all notions of reality and truth, but also to displace the autonomous ego from its false pretensions to mastery and certainty. In that sense, the linguistic turn of modern thought bears enormous political and social consequences. Prevailing notions of a purely autonomous self must go. It matters little whether that ego takes on the studied smile of resason of the Enlightenment, the volcanic passion of the romantic, or arid self-satisfaction of the positivist, or the mature complacency of much modern psychology.

Whether we know it or not, we are all de-centered egos now.[8] We are all linguistic, historical, social beings struggling for some new interpretations of ourselves, our language, history, society, and culture. The linguistic turn has not been solely an intellectual movement. Wittgenstein's sketching of the plurality of language games and the plurality of forms of life freed much Anglo-American philosophy from the seductions of positivism. Heidegger's more gnomic utterances on "language as the house of being" helped to free much Continental philosphy from idealist and romantic self-interpretations. Both Wittgenstein and Heidegger, despite their other major differences, de-centered the modern self and challenged the now-strained humanist belief that humans are the measure of all things.[9]

To enter the linguistic turn in philosophy is, in principle, to reenter history and society. But that reentry has been impeded by various strategies of disengagement from the often-harsh realities of history. This is the case even with Wittgenstein and Heidegger themselves. It is puzzling how lacking in interest Wittgenstein was in the historical development of the very language games and forms of life he analyzed. Heidegger dismissed the public realm as mere curiosity, ambiguity, and chatter. How, then, could we expect him to appreciate Hannah Arendt's work on the public realm?[10] Did he really understand the significance of his own withdrawal from history to the clearings of Being in the Black Forest? Unfortunately, the acknowledgement of the linguistic character of all understanding can become an occasion for passivity in the face of what history is, what it has been, or what it might become. We may well live in "a time-in-between." We do need to learn again what Heidegger taught—to listen and to wait.[11] But can we do only that?

The analysis of the ineradicable plurality of languages and forms of life was the singular contribution of Wittgenstein. The insistence that every disclosure is at the same time a disclosure and a concealment, since Being always both reveals and withdraws itself in every manifestation: this was the unique achievement of the late Heidegger. The history of effects of both Wittgenstein and Heidegger and, increasingly, of both together has affected contemporary understandings of interpretation as both active and passive. The plural possibilities of an active understanding of language have been accelerated. Wittgenstein's analysis of the social nature of all understanding showed the "family resemblances" not only among various language games but also among different forms of life. His analyses illuminated even those most important of language games, the games of "certainty" that every culture uses for its most basic beliefs and practices.[12] For Heidegger, the insistence upon the historicity of all understanding was always central.[13]

Both thinkers concentrated on the inescapable reality of language as well as on our plural uses of it and its uses of us. They insisted upon such plurality, to be sure, in very different ways: in Wittgenstein through a description of the radical plurality of language games; in Heidegger through the normative insistence on authentic languages, such as poetry, as distinct from inauthentic, even fallen, languages, such as the onto-theo-logical language of traditional metaphysics. Indeed, for Heidegger these inauthentic languages included the fallen languages of publicness as well as the languages of calculative thought as opposed to meditative thought.[14] Heidegger's plurality may seem more limited than Wittgenstein's, but in one sense it is more radical. For Heidegger, as for his mentor Heraclitus, plurality and difference are always present in all authentic speech. Radical difference cannot be eliminated. Indeed, difference itself is that unnameable that is always different from itself and thereby from any language of presence that attempts to state it. All is articulated through difference, and nothing can ever reduce that difference to a statement of pure presence and identity.[15]

Both Heidegger and Wittgenstein gave normative status to one mode of discourse above all others—silence.[16] This trust in silence may explain both their deep respect for the mystical and their otherwise puzzling lack of interest in the realities of history, suggested by both Heidegger's analysis of historicity and Wittgenstein's analysis of the forms of life.

Wittgenstein and Heidegger remain the two great modern masters of the analysis of language, knowledge, and reality. Despite their radical differences, they are strangely complementary influences. However, there is a third master who founded both a new way to understand language systemically and the new discipline of linguistics for that study: Ferdinand de Saussure.[17] Saussure was interested, above all, in language as a system. He elaborated a scientific but not scientistic way to study language. In relation to the categories considered thus far, Saussure and his successors introduced another and crucial interruption in the interpretation of language. For linguistics, first in Saussure, then in modern structuralism and semiotics, confronts any analysis of the use of language with a theory of language as system.[18]

What is striking in the development of Saussure's insights is not solely its particular fruitfulness in the explanatory theories of structuralist thinkers like Lévi-Strauss. Rather, it is this paradox: Saussurean linguistics comes dressed in scientific garb. Nevertheless, these linguistic, synchronic theories finally demonstrate as great a plurality within language as that sugggested by earlier analyses of language as use. Indeed, this plurality functions not only in Saussure's own thought but, above all, in the challenge to, and the radicalization of, Saussure by the poststructuralism of Jacques Derrida and others.

Besides the analyses of language use in classical philosophy, in historical studies, in analytical philosophy, and in hermeneutical philosophy, there is the analysis of language as a system. This is made possible by distinguishing between synchronic analyses of language as a system of differentially related signs and diachronic analyses of language as it has been used historically. Any analysis of use, as we saw above, shows the social and historical character of all languages. But synchronic analysis chooses to forgo historical studies of the development of language in favor of a more systemic approach.

Such a synchronic theory provides an important interruption which can lead in several directions. For example, conversation, after all, is discourse: "someone says something to someone about something."[19] When discourse exists, language must function as use. But in order to function at all, language must also be a system of differentiated signs. *Discourse* is a word used by Benveniste to insist that language, properly speaking, is both system (*langue*) and use (*parole*).[20] All synchronic analyses are, therefore, relevant to discourse analysis. All analyses of language as use—including all studies of the individual, cultural, historical, and ethical-political uses of any word, sentence, or text— are also relevant to discourse analysis. As Benveniste and Ricoeur have argued, the move from language as system to language as discourse should be a move through, not around, an analysis of language as system. If any analysis of language as systemic object is not to become one more scientistic attempt to avoid history and society, then linguistics should of course interrupt earlier analyses of the uses of language but not replace them. This, at least as I interpret it, was also the unfulfilled ideal of Saussure himself.[21] It is clearly the ideal of any modern discourse analyst.

In the case of linguistics, theory has proved once again fruitful for understanding.[22] For through linguistic theory we learn that language can also be interpreted synchronically, that is, as a system (*langue*) abstracted from particular speech acts (*parole*). Hence language is understood as it functions at any particular fixed point in time. Language can then be described as a system of differential relations. To clarify this move, let us note the example of *tree*. *Tree* has the meaning it does only by means of its *differences* from all other signs—*free* or *three* in graphemes; or *she*, *be*, or *thee* in sound images. On this model, meaning in language is not immanent in the sign *tree*. Meaning is always functional.

At its emergence in the signifiers of language, meaning is the result of the differences of this sign from all other signs. This position is in notable contrast to classical discussions of universals as well as any Cartesian or Husserlian yearnings for a full presence immanent to purely unitary signs. In Saussure's most famous and interruptive formulation, "In the linguistic system there are only differences."[23] Thus linguistics studies the system of signs (*langue*) that makes all speech possible, not the actual use of speech by particular speakers in particular situations (*parole*).

These studies have also influenced interpretation theory. As a positive contribution, linguistics had challenged empiricist, Platonist, and romantic notions of signs, symbols, and experiences. Other contributions of these studies of language as a system remain subject to controversy. The major controversy is about which aspects of Saussurean analysis one agrees with, presumably for good linguistic reasons, and which aspects one disagrees with, again for good linguistic reasons. As a result, there are three major alternatives in post-Saussurean hermeneutics.

For the first clue to the alternatives involved, we must return to Saussure's major claim: "In the linguistic *system*, there are only *differences*" (my emphasis). If the systemic factor is highlighted over against the differential, one finds various formulations or structuralist, formalist, and semiotic analyses. Structuralist analyses, for example (here Lévi-Strauss on myths is exemplary), typically develop Saussure's own position by building on what he said on sign systems, of which *langue* is one.[24] Structuralists and semioticians attend to subject matters other than the original analysis of language itself. Signs and structures mean both language in the usual linguistic sense and all signs, including such cultural signs as symbols and myths and their systemic structures. At the limit, synchronic analysis applies to the deep structures of all reality, including history itself. Structuralists and semioticians attempt, like ancient grammarians, to uncover the basic units of various sign systems, such as Lévi-Strauss's "mythemes." These basic structures and signs are directly analogous to the basic units of sounds called phonemes in alphabetic languages. Hence structuralists analyze how these units combine, for example, by means of certain fundamental binary oppositions such as high-low, raw-cooked, and so on. Systemic binary oppositions, it is further claimed, produce the transformative linguistic effects we call by such names as myths and narratives. The debates within such grammatical enterprises as structuralism and semiotics are both vigorous and important. For present purposes, however, it is sufficient to note that structuralism, semiotics, and such other formal analyses as Propp's *Morphology of Folk-Tales* are all basically new grammatical enterprises built upon modern systemic explanatory theories. Yet, like all good grammatical analyses, these theories also show how various basic oppositions, combinations, and transformations of these differentially related signs or elements function to produce mythical meanings (Lévi-Strauss), poetic meanings (Jakobson), and narrative meanings (Genette or the early Barthes).[25]

Modern structuralist and semiotic methods encourage a demythologizing of some favored humanist concepts: empiricist complacency with experience; romantic effusiveness about symbols; historicist self-satisfaction on relating all reality to either a historical origin or a historical telos; humanist self-congratulations on their grounding of all reality in the human. Whether these systemic methods can fulfill their promise to account for all reality through their explanatory theories is, however, another question. In fact, it is several questions. In one sense, the argument between structuralists and poststructuralists (the latter including deconstructionists like Derrida and discourse analysts like Benveniste and Ricoeur, or even that analyst of anonymous discourses, Foucault) is a replay of the ancient arguments between grammarians and rhetoricians. The argument can be posed in two principal ways. First, is it possible to account for the actual persuasive use of language (rhetoric) by analyzing only the structural relationships and codes of transformation (grammar) that provide the conditions of possibility for all good language use? Second, is it possible to divorce grammatical analyses of language from rhetorical analyses without finding, at the end of the analysis, that the rhetorical tropes were there all along? Do the tropes not operate behind one's back as signs of the forces that increase, rather than eliminate, difference, conflict, and rupture within the system? As Derrida states, "What I can never understand, in a structure, is that by means of which it is not closed."[26]

To begin with the second question: in one sense, deconstructive thought is the most recent invasion of grammar by rhetoric, more exactly, the destabilizing rhetoric of the tropes.[27] In more linguistic terms, structuralists are concerned to expand and solidify the systemic gains of Saussurean analysis. They need not deny the differential character of signs. But by analyzing the grammatical transformations functioning in the relations of binary oppositions, they believe they can show how the fundamental structures constitute an internally self-referential system. Poststructuralism of a deconstructive bent counters this claim with an insistence on the original Saussurean insight into the arbitrariness, the differences, the supplementary character, and the dispersing of meanings produced by signs. The original quasislogan "In the linguistic system, there are only differences" will now not read "In the linguistic *system*, there are only differences," but "In the linguistic system, there are *only differences.*"

Deconstructionists challenge all claims to uncovering the fully systemic character of any language by insisting upon the implications of the fact that no system can adequately account for its own ineradicably differential nature. The self-enclosed systems of differential relations in structuralist thought then yield to self-deconstructing antisystems, antihierarchies, and antiidentity.[28] Indeed, Derrida holds that even Saussure and Lévi-Strauss, despite their insight into the arbitrary character of the functional relationships between signifier and signified and the conventional character of their relationship to referents, still hoped for some grounding identity of self-present meaning through either system or structure or unitary sign.[29] Saussure's hope took the form of an unexamined belief that signifier and signified, though not referent, somehow formed a synchronic unity that rendered meaning self-consciously present. But such unity is called into question by Saussure's own analysis of the arbitrariness of the relationships between signifier and signified or concept, and thereby the purely differential character of meaning. As Saussure himself demonstrated, a word like *tree* means "tree" only by being *different* from *she* or *be* or *thee* (in sounds) or *free* or *three* (in graphemes). *Tree* means "tree" by *not* being *free, three, be, thee, she,* and so forth. A word can mean only through its relationships of difference among the signifiers. The traces of these absent signifiers must, therefore, be always already present/absent to this signifier *tree* in order for *tree* to have any meaning at all.

After such radical differentiality, what unitary system? What hierarchical structure? After such knowledge, what consolation for any full presence of meaning in any unitary sign?

In sum, for poststructuralists, meaning functions along the whole chain of signifiers. We never in fact reach a unitary meaning purely present to itself as a sign freed from all the differences needed to produce the meaning. No sign, on Saussure's own analysis, is free from the traces of other officially absent signifiers. The traces of those absent signifiers must operate through the whole differential system ad infinitum for any sign to have meaning at all.

Where Saussure placed his hopes on the unitary sign, Lévi-Strauss placed his on a unitary structure. But the same nonreducible play of differences, ruptures, traces of absent signifiers, the same radical dissemination of all signifiers also interrupts this hope for a self-enclosed system.[30] The system does not, for it cannot as a "system" of differences, ever fully systematize itself. It cannot, for the system itself is made materially of the same play of signifying differences which is language. Any hope for a full "presence" of meaning is, for Derrida, the most characteristic gesture of Western logocentric thought. This illusory hope is most clearly exposed in Western prejudices against writing interpreted as the absence of living—that is, self-present—speech in the living present, not only in Plato but also in Saussure, Lévi-Strauss, and Husserl.[31] But, for Derrida, these modern grammarians (Saussureans, formalists, semioticians, eidetic phenomenologists, and structuralists) cannot be allowed to deny their own repressed insight: the always already radically differential character of all signs, all structures, all systems; the illusory character of all implied claims (Lévi-Strauss) or explicit claims (Descartes, Husserl) to a nonlinguistic pure self-presence of consciousness. In Derrida's view, we need to break the link between signifier and signified itself—the last link by means of which these modern structuralist grammarians could try to hold at bay the diffusive, rupturing, disseminating, differential, deconstructing play of differences in their own discourse.

Derrida has become the Trojan horse in the camp of the structuralists. But a very un-Greek horse he is. For our Western problems begin, he insists, with the logocentric, phonocentric, and phallocentric prejudices of our Greek forebears.[32] The Greeks believed that consciousness can be present to itself, he thinks, in every present moment of speech. They wanted Plato's *pharmakon* but refused to admit that it is always already both medicine and poison.[33] In Derrida's scenario, we will do almost anything to assure ourselves that we possess self-presence. By sleight of hand, we pretend that, even if the referent is related to the sign only by convention, somehow the signifier and signified form an indissoluble unity. We continue to hope that all narratives, myths, and cultures can be reduced to a system of binary oppositions and rules of transformation.

Yet it would be a mistake to read Derrida's attack upon structuralism as a retreat from Sausurrean and structuralist insights, much less as a defense of humanist or romantic interpretations of language and self-presence. On the contrary, Derrida radicalizes the Saussurean insights into language as constituted by *differential* relations. He capitalizes on Saussure's confusing comments on writing and his admission of the arbitrariness of the links between signifier and signified. No more than Lévi-Strauss does Derrida wish to rehabilitate positivist notions of science, historicist notions of history, empiricist notions of experience, or romantic notions of symbol. Derrida merits the designation poststructuralist. Above all, Derrida joins Lévi-Strauss and all structuralists in exposing the illusory character of the self portrayed as a self-present user of language as instrument, the self as a reality-founding ego. For this ego is never fully present to itself—not even in Descartes's moments of certainty or Husserl's transcendental reduction. Indeed, the modern Cartesian ego has collided with its own language use only to awaken and not know who, or what, it is.[34] The ego is now de-centered. The dream of full presence is no more. Synchronically our language turns out to be an unrealizable system of differences. When we use language, moreover, we must always defer any claims to full meaning, for the differences multiply and the traces of absent meanings are disseminated. We must both differ and defer in order for meaning to happen at all. Words, in this Derridean vision, begin to dissolve into their signifiers, and the signifiers disperse all meaning. All is difference, and all difference is always already a deferral of full meaning. Difference has become *différance*.[35]

As was the case with the Venetian ambassador of the Elizabethan drama, when Jacques Derrida enters, the conversation stops. With his brilliant rococo theories, he seems to insinuate himself into all conversations. And after the entry of the ambassador of Venice, no one is ever quite sure what the conversation was—or even whether there was one. Yet Venice had its aims. So too does Derrida. His maritime policy is to produce a rhetoric of radical destabilization to expose any pretensions to full self-presence, any self-congratulatory Western resting in an untroubled, alinguistic, self-present, grounding ego.

Our knowledge of reality is irrevocably linked to our use of language. Our use of language is possible because of the differential relations that constitute the words of the particular language. Any claims to full presence, especially claims to full self-presence in conscious thought, are illusions that cannot survive a study of language as a system of differential relations. Like a Zen master, Derrida has exposed an illusion, the illusion that we language-sated beings can ever be fully present to ourselves or that any other reality can be fully present to us either.[36] All grammars and logics seem to become unstable and plural in the presence of this radical rhetoric let loose within grammar and logic themselves. Even hermeneutics can seem to be undone from within.[37] If all is difference, can any genuine conversation or even argument occur? For Derrida all argument is determined rhetorically, and by rhetoric he does not mean the rhetoric of the topics but the uncanny rhetoric of the tropes. In that event, can any argument win? After the interruption of the linguistic trajectory from Saussure to Derrida, the hope for both conversation and argument may seem in vain. But is it?

A transcendental "tu quoque" argument against Derrida is not inappropriate but will not suffice.[38] For Derrida not only knows, he insists, that he too is caught up in the indeterminable plurality and difference in all our phonetic Western languages and consequently in all our interpretations of language, consciousness, knowledge, and reality. Derrida's rhetoric is one with a Utopian tone and a strange note of ironic ultimacy: the "abyss of indeterminacy" that is our situation, the text outside of which nothing exists. An anarchic pleasure in the free play of language pervades much deconstructive rhetoric of unending irony. Deconstructive criticism, despite its self-descriptions, suggests certain general (transcendental?) characteristics of language, knowledge, and reality.[39]

But deconstructive analyses are not put forward to ground a situation; rather they are meant to function as linguistic therapy. They expose certain fundamental illusions in our familiar accounts of knowledge, reality, and language. The illusion that we could separate how we know reality from language had already collapsed in the earlier therapeutic stages of the linguistic turn. But with the entry of that third modern master of the linguistic turn, Saussure, it seemed to some that a turn from language as use to language as system could stabilize the ever-increasing plurality. But here Derrida's contribution is helpful, for the developments of structuralist and poststructuralist studies of language have exposed as illusory the hope that any full-presenced unity of meaning already lost through hermeneutical analyses of actual language use could be retrieved by studying language as systemic object. The anlaysis of the plurality of language use by Wittgenstein and the interpretation of the plurality in every disclosure of language by Heidegger have now been joined by the analysis of Derrida on the plurality within language as an object of differential relations. Whether or not language becomes discourse in Derrida himself is a genuine puzzle. For all his writing on writing and textuality, and for all his brilliant deconstructive analyses of classic texts like Rousseau, what is Derrida's real interest in texts? His typical strategy, and his contribution, seems less directed at texts than at individual words such as *supplément* within texts.[40]

But texts are not dictionaries. In texts, words do not have meaning on their own. There are sentences, paragraphs, chapters, books—there are texts. There are composition, genre, style as strategies of producing meaning in the text. There is none of that in words alone. Even those Western masters of the materiality of words and sounds, the rabbis and the kabbalists, interpreted single words in order to illuminate not single words alone but texts—especially The Text. Derrida, as his essay on Jabes hints, may prefer to be a poet, a "laughing rabbi" (Reb Rida), rather than a rabbi, an interpreter of texts.[41] But his laughing rush to the de-centering words in every text may finally force him to find himself in an echo chamber of words alone—which, ironically, are all there is "outside the text."

To insist that the analysis of language move past words to sentences and eventually to texts is to insist that language is neither system alone nor use alone, but discourse.[42] In discourse, "someone says something about something to someone." That someone may be the commonsensical meaning of someone. Or it may be an extended meaning—as when we spoke above of the text's claim to our attention. That someone may be Heidegger's "they" with their inauthentic speech. That someone may even be Lacan's "ça parle." The "about something" may be a relatively straightforward message such as that occasioned by the green light at a traffic stop. It may be found in as multivoiced a text as *The Idiot*[43] or as labyrinthine a rendering of "something" as *The Turn of the Screw*. Across the whole spectrum of someones, somethings, and about somethings, we find words, sentences, paragraphs, texts. We find discourse.

To discover discourse is to explore language as a reality beyond individual words in the dictionary, beyond both synchronic codes (*langue*) and individual use of words (*parole*); it is to rediscover society and history. Every discourse expresses conscious and unconscious ideologies, whether the someone who speaks or writes is aware of them or not. For example, my own discourse in this book expresses ideologies of which I may or may not be aware but which any good discourse analyst of ideologies can spot. We have in this chapter moved from an interpretation of language as use, to language as system, to language as differential nonsystem, and now to discourse. To acknowledge that language is discourse is to admit the need for ethical and political criticism of the hidden, even repressed, social and historical ideologies in all texts, in all langauge as discourse, and, above all, in all interpretations.

To lose any belief in pure self-presence as well as any claims to certainty or to apodictic knowledge is not to deny the possibility of knowledge itself. What we know, we know with relative adequacy, and we know it is bounded by the realities of language, society, and history. On any particular issue, we can know when we have no further relevant questions. It is possible, therefore, to know when we know enough.

If we want more than that, we will be tempted to believe in an illusion, the illusion that our total and immediate presence to ourselves is the ground of reality—a reality now without language, without society, and without history. But we can have relatively adequate knowledge, better interpretations, verified possibilities, and judicious discourse whenever we use language well. And all these can be informed by the various rhetorics of ultimacy that the linguistic turn, in all its permutations, has achieved. Indeed, a rhetoric of the indeterminacy and plurality of the tropes can inform, and, in many cases, transform, every rhetoric of topical argument and every hermeneutic of conversation. But that rhetoric too, precisely as rhetoric, attempts to persuade us to the truth. Short of fiat, however, a rhetoric of the tropes cannot simply replace persuasive argument and conversation. Deconstructive criticism also lives by its uses, good and bad arguments informing its practice and theories as well as relevant and irrelevant uses of those practices and theories in its readings. If we are not to retreat from what the early stages of the linguistic turn taught us—the inevitability of the realities of history and society in all language—then we must, at some point, turn from an interpretation of language-as-object back to an interpretation of language-as-use. We must turn from the deconstruction of words to a chastened interpretation of texts. Indeed, at its best, deconstructive criticism is also discourse.

Deconstructive writers, after all, are not in the business of writing dictionaries. They write texts. Meaning may disperse endlessly through the signifiers of all our words. But meaning is also crystalized into significant discourse by sentences, paragraphs, chapters, and texts—including deconstructive texts. And all texts, theirs and mine, are saturated with the ideologies of particular societies, the history of ambiguous effects of particular traditions, and the hidden agendas of the unconscious.

The favorite illusion of some deconstructionist thinkers is that they have so freed themselves from history and society that they alone can enjoy the energizing experience of language deconstructing itself. But this is at least as familiar an illusion of Western intellectuals as any claim to full self-presence. It is an illusion challenged by their own rhetorizing of structuralist grammar. It is the illusion that history and society can be kept at bay while we all enjoy the surf of the signifiers. But history and society do not wait upon us. History and society engulf us even as we speak and write. Whether we notice or not, society and history are always already there. They are there every time "someone says something to someone about something." They are there every time some deconstructive thinker says or writes something about signifiers to someone. They are there every time another aporia of Western thought is spotted. Hedonism, skepticism, and epicureanism are familiar and honorable responses of some Western intellectuals to particular societies in certain moments of their histories. But as much as all other ethical-political options, they too must argue their case, as Seneca did.

Language as a system of differential relations makes possible any actual use of language, and consequently all knowledge of reality. Language as discourse should make use of the knowledge attained by structuralist and poststructuralist thought. The third trajectory of the linguistic turn moves, therefore, in a more explicitly hermeneutical direction by means of explicit discourse analysis. In technical terms, this may be described as the movement from language as use (step one), to language as object (step two), to language as discourse (step three). The practicioners of this last step include such disparate and conflicting thinkers as Michel Foucault, Jacques Lacan, Michel de Certeau, Julia Kristeva, Frederic Jameson, Edward Said, Emil Benveniste, and Paul Ricoeur.[44] To employ the word discourse in this sense is to suggest that one need not simply return to a pre-Saussurean position. Rather, as we have seen above, there are good reasons to make the interruptive detour through structuralist and poststructuralist studies of language. Like all arguments and like all explanatory theories based on sound arguments, these studies have challenged previous forms of interpretation. These studies have challenged hermeneutical interpretations of language, such as Heidegger's "short route" to ontology and Gadamer's "short route" to hermeneutics through conversation with the tradition. These studies have also called into question some unexamined claims of Anglo-American linguistic analysis by rethinking both language as system and the rhetoric of the tropes in language as use.[45] Hence our choices are not limited to linguistic and hermeneutical analyses of actual language use or to structuralist, semiotic, and poststructuralist analyses of language as a system of differential relations. Rather, as any interpreter of language, knowledge, and reality moves past the level of words to texts, concern with actual language use returns in a new way.

Discourse analysis demands a study of movement from words to sentences to texts, through an explanatory study of each of these levels of increasing linguistic complexity. Notice, for example, Ricoeur's study of metaphor on the level of sentences, not mere words, as well as his companion study of the role of plot for narratives.[46] All analyses willing to undertake a journey through the explanatory theories of linguistics, and not around them, are discourse analyses. Foucault, for example, was correct to resist the label "structuralist" even for his early work on anonymous discourses.[47] He was also correct to resist the label "hermeneute" if the latter implied, as it sometimes does, an antiexplanatory stance. But Foucault was, indeed, a discourse anlayst: more exactly, a poststructuralist interpreter of the power of pervasive but anonymous discourses, especially of the complex relations between power and truth in all discourses. Lacan was correct to resist the easy interpretation that he had simply applied Saussure's linguistics to Freud's texts. It is more accurate to say that Lacan executed a hermeneutical retrieval of the uncanny otherness of Freud's own discovery of the unconscious, by reading Freudian texts as discourse. In this reading, Lacan both returns to and rethinks Freud to the point where he can then suggest that "the unconscious is structured like a language." Then and probably only then, he insists, can we realize that the play of the signifiers in the unconscious de-centers the ego of much revisionist Freudian theory.

Lacan's own discourse, with its convoluted prose, is well geared to resist the illusory clarity of much writing on Freud.[48] However rigorously descriptive and explanatory the discourse analyses of Foucault, Lacan, and Ricoeur are, an ethical-political tone also pervades their texts. In fact, they can be rightly considered as the contemporary heirs of the classic French moralist tradition from Montaigne through Pascal to Camus. An ethical-political voice may also be heard, though in a more muted form, in many other poststructuralist writers. If our situation is as radically ironic as Paul de Man seems to suggest, then let this be made explicit and argued for as the ethical-political choice we should all make.[49] If, as Roland Barthes suggests, we should abandon the too earnest duty-bound task of hermeneutics in favor of an "erotics of reading," then this, too, can be made rhetorically persuasive. If explicit argument is too earnest and bourgeois, Barthes had at his comand the means to persuade. What other text possesses so rare a combination of almost irresistible charm and seductive *aperçus* as his *The Pleasure of the Text*?[50] Any rhetoric of ultimacy, even Derrida's almost Zenlike rhetoric on the radical abyss of indeterminacy (emptiness?), influences our motivations to act or not to act. Once we leave purely formal analyses—and all discourse analysis shows that we are always already leaving it—we find ourselves in history and society.[51] There are many reasons to be attracted to poststructuralist thought. I have tried to indicate some of them above. There are even better reasons, I have also suggested, to make use of modern hermeneutical discourse analysis, which is, after all, only a modern return to, and rethinking of, both ancient rhetoric and earlier hermeneutics.

We do not need more of the same. We do not need a new monism. With Foucault we need to begin to examine all "that goes without saying." More than Foucault himself suggests, we should learn new strategies of resistance. We should defend differences and plurality. We should explore possibilities without allowing every one of them to fall victim to the exigencies of purely formal argument. When we turn to argument, we need, above all, arguments that take their own topical and substantive character seriously. We need to converse with one another on the ethical-political implications of all analyses of language and reality. We need to enter history again, but to enter it alert to all that those studies of language have to teach us.

To study language as discourse is to discover plurality. It is also to rediscover the contingency and ambiguity of history and society. To study grammar and rhetoric is also to discover plurality and to rediscover with the ancients that the ethical and the political are one. Among competing visions of the good life, how can we decide on the most relatively adequate one for responsible action? It is possible to defend plurality by finding better ways to fight against the reign of more of the same and to affirm the reality of difference. But can that affirmation be sustained if we do not face the "nightmare from which we are trying to awake," history itself?

CHAPTER 4

Radical Ambiguity: The Question of History

To interpret language is to find oneself in the contingent reality named history. To be in history is to be born, live, and die bounded by a particular sex, race, class, and education. To acquire a native language is to acquire the means to articulate thought and feeling in a manner native to a particular history. Every language carries a range of values, hopes, and prejudices that function preconsciously when native speakers hear certain words. *"Liberté, égalité, fraternité"* carries a powerful history of effects for any native speaker of French, just as "life, liberty, and the pursuit of happiness" carries strong resonances for any American speaker of English. We are inevitably shaped by the history we were born into. With critical thought, responsible actions, and some luck, we may help to change history in some small measure. Our history is the way it is not because of any natural necessity but only because equally historical individuals have struggled before us.

Language and history are indissolubly bound. Speakers of English are now aware that the words *man* and *mankind* do not serve to encompass all humankind. Once vibrant words can die the death of a thousand qualifications. Words can even fall victim to historical violence. How differently our eighteenth-century ancestors used the words *sentiment, the sublime,* and *virtue.* Consider such relatively recent arrivals as the words *literature* and *culture,* or such politically potent words as *right* and *left.*[1] Today these last two words continue to shift their meanings as rapidly as in the Terror the political parties in the Revolutionary Assembly kept moving their places from left to right enroute to the guillotine.

Although we do belong to language and history more than they belong to us, we should be wary of using too easily such words as *belong* and *participate*.[2] We must confront the interruptions embedded in our history, for, however paradoxically, we also belong to those interruptions. Voltaire's reaction to Damien's attempted assassination of Louis XV is interesting in this regard: "How could such a thing happen in these enlightened times? One's blood freezes!"[3] As we read Voltaire's letter further, we realize that it was the thought of an assassination attempt on the king that was so shocking, not the public spectacle of the torture and killing of the failed assassin. That seemed both natural and necessary—even to Voltaire!

We, on the other hand, in a century that has witnessed too many successful and unsuccessful assassination attempts to be shocked, find Damien's attempt unremarkable.[4] But we may be taken aback in reading accounts of the public spectacle of his torture and death and perhaps shocked at the complacent silence of even the humane Voltaire. But have we the right to our shock?

The thought of the complacency of early nineteenth-century England in the face of the appalling fate of young chimney sweeps can haunt us as much as it provoked Blake into writing his great poem.[5] In our own century we can contemplate what? More of the same. The genocide of six million Jews by the Nazis is—is what? *Shocking* seems an altogether inadequate adjective to apply to that enormity. Then what was it? Madness? Aberration? Sin? Or all these, and something more, something demonic and more radically interruptive of our history than we can imagine? The Holocaust is a searing interruption of all the traditions in Western culture. None of us yet know even how to name it properly. This much, however, is clear: if we continue to talk about our history as if that *tremendum* event did not happen, then we are not truthfully narrating our history.[6] And our century includes that and more. Witness the following litany of terrifying events: the Armenian massacres, the Gulag, Hiroshima, Uganda, and Cambodia. We must recognize that Western humanist history includes the guards at Auschwitz who read

Goethe and listened to Bach and Mozart in their "spare time."[7] Such behavior cannot be just another fact to fit into a developmental history of Western enlightenment.

History is not only contingent; history is interruptive.[8] Western history is, through and through, an interruptive narrative with no single theme and no controlling plot. To be an American, for example, is to live with pride by participating in a noble experiment of freedom and plurality. But to be a white American is also to belong to a history that encompasses the near destruction of one people (the North American Indians, the true native Americans) and the enslavement of another people (the blacks). Not to honor the ancient Greeks as our ancestors is possible only for those who lack any sense of true greatness. But to honor and belong to the Greeks is also to recognize the interruptions in their, that is, our, history: the role of the other as barbarian, the vindictive policies of imperialist Athens towards Melos and other colonies, the unexamined role of women and slaves in the polis, the cries of the Athenians themselves in the quarries of Syracuse.[9]

Indeed, the more one reads and loves our greatest Western classics—the Hebrew and Christian Scriptures, the Greeks, the Romans, and all their later descendants, the more their true claim to our attention becomes like the claim to attention of Greek tragedy itself.[10] Those plays concentrate one's attention by their undeniable power and greatness. They stir one's conscience with their demands for nobility of thought and action. They expose our present inauthenticity and complacency. At the same time, they also force us to resist their own half-concealed tragic flaws.

When we risk genuine conversation with the classics, it can become too easy to rattle off the usual list of hidden skeletons in the Western closet—those systemic "isms" that we sometimes know, more often sense, through some discomfort that afflicts us: sexism, racism, classism, elitism, cultural parochialism.[11] To claim the ancient Israelites as our predecessors is an honor. But that claim also forces us to face the patriarchal nature of their society.[12] We cannot forget what the Israelites did to the Canaanites and what their prayers against the children of their enemies might mean. To cherish the Christian scriptures as a charter document of liberation is entirely right. Yet we must also face its anti-Judaic strands, strands that reach us with the full history of the effects of centuries of Christian "teaching of contempt" for the Jews.[13] And we have just begun to face the centuries of subjugation of women in Christian history—indeed, in all Western history.

To see how ambiguous our history has been, however, is not simply to retire into that more subtle mode of complacency, universal and ineffectual guilt. Rather, as Abraham Joshua Heschel insisted: "Not all are guilty but all are responsible." Responsible here means capable of responding: capable of facing the interruptions in our history; capable of discarding any scenarios of innocent triumph written, as always, by the victors; capable of not forgetting the subversive memories of individuals and whole peoples whose names we do not even know. If we attempt such responses, we are making a beginning—and only a beginning—in assuming historical responsibility.

To risk conversation with our classic texts should be more like meeting such characters as Amos and Isaiah, Ruth and Jeremiah, Oedipus and Antigone, even Medea and Herakles, than it is like conceiving the classics simply as further examples of ideology. To suspect the presence of ideology is one thing. To face the actuality of the ideologies in ourselves and even in our most beloved classics is quite another. Our best critical theories, on this reading, should always inform our readings of the classics but not be allowed to take over that conversation. We make things too easy for ourselves if classic texts become nothing more than occasions to illustrate general theory. We do not need to converse with Job's comforters or his critics. We are all too familiar with them in ourselves. We need to face Job. Resistance to the classics can also be as necessary a response in any conversation with them as any recognition of their greatness. Any method, any theory of interpretation, any argument can aid that conversation. But none can replace it.

No classic text comes to us without the plural and ambiguous history of effects of its own production and all its former receptions.[14] Nor does any classic event, be it the Renaissance, the Reformation, or the Enlightenment. "Every great work of civilization," as Walter Benjamin insisted, "is at the same time a work of barbarism." Plurality seems an adequate word to suggest the extraordinary variety that any study of language shows, and any study of the variety of receptions of any classic documents. Ambiguity may be too mild a word to describe the strange mixture of great good and frightening evil that our history reveals. And yet, at least until more adequate and probably new words are coined, ambiguity will have to suffice.[15]

Historical ambiguity means that a once seemingly clear historical narrative of progressive Western enlightenment and emancipation has now become a montage of classics and newspeak, of startling beauty and revolting cruelty, of partial emancipation and ever-subtler forms of entrapment. Ambiguous is certainly one way to describe our history. At one time we may have believed realistic and even naturalistic narratives of the triumph of the West.[16] But these traditional narratives are now overlaid not only with modernist narratives and their occasional epiphanies amidst the mass of historical confusion, but also by postmodernist antinarratives with their good-byes to all that.[17]

There are many scholarly ways to reflect on the writing of history.[18] One can analyze the epistemology of historiography; compare nineteenth-century notions of historical consciousness with twentieth-century concepts of historicity; develop comparative analyses of the relative strengths and weaknesses of different speculative philosophies and theologies of history; or analyze whether history itself is best understood as event or as structure.

What we also need, however—and what fortunately we possess—is contemporary historians producing works of history that speak forcefully to our need to understand our various pasts as we negotiate the possibilities of our present and future. Their work ranges from detailed analyses of a single period or person, to the recovery of forgotten events, individuals, and peoples, to reinterpretations of a whole age. A good historian, perhaps more than any other thinker or artist, can most clearly demonstrate the truth of the observation that though life is reflected upon through general ideas, it is always lived in the details; witness Ladurie's fascinating studies of everyday life in a single village in medieval France; or Walter Jackson Bate's extraordinary biography of Doctor Johnson, that quintessential English genius of common sense who mastered the art of living in all its plural and ambiguous detail.[19]

Other historians command our attention by their ability to

help us to face the interruptions and otherness in our histories and in ourselves. In particular, feminist historians are retrieving and writing the history of women, the most systematically repressed "others" in all of our male-dominated histories.[20] Still other historians have contributed to this historical interest in the archaeology of the "other" by their pioneering studies of peoples and categories of peoples who have until now suffered the fate of often being ignored.[21] Eugene Genovese in his *Roll Jordan Roll: The World the Slaves Made*, John Boswell in his *Christianity, Social Tolerance, and Homosexuality*, and Frances Yates in her *The Rosicrucian Enlightenment* have successfully retrieved some aspects of the history of previously ignored categories of persons. Sometimes we are even surprised to discover that a people and a society that were widely assumed to be more of the same are genuinely other, as in Manning Clark's masterful portrayal of the history of aboriginal and immigrant European peoples become a unique national culture, Australia.

Besides these histories of previously marginalized people and peoples, another, although less particular category, has found its historians. The work of George Rudé and Richard Cobb on the French Revolution has focused attention not on the ideas and singular characters and events of that revolution but on the ultimate bearers of its meaning, as indeed of the meaning of all history, the people.[22]

Fortunately, that great tradition of historical writing to which the classics of Burckhardt and de Tocqueville belong is still alive in the work of such historians as Arnaldo Momigliano, with his commanding studies of the ancient world, and Hans Blumenberg, with his magisterial studies of modernity.[23] This tradition, which finds its sources in the classic histories of Herodotus and Thucydides, Plutarch, Livy, Tacitus, and even Suetonius, continues to provide us, particularly in fresh readings and appraisal, with the necessary other perspectives on our own times. Whoever is tired of historical works such as these, is, to borrow Dr. Johnson's famous comment on London, tired of life.

The good, the true, the beautiful, and the holy are present in our history. As I have argued throughout this work, these realities need continual retrieval by unrelenting conversation with all the great classics.[24] But we are in dire need of new strategies for facing the interruptions of radical evil in our history.

What kind of conversation can aid us here? What kind of arguments will help?

As before, so too here, the search should not be for the one and only way to move forward. Rather, in keeping with the pluralistic strategy defended so far, we can say again with Kenneth Burke, "Use all that can be used." Here too we can discover or invent new strategies to carry forward the struggle for some emancipation and some enlightenment. We can develop new and more complex narratives that elicit the subversive memories of those individuals and peoples whose stories have been distorted by the compulsive narratives of the Faustian victors. We should abandon any narratives empowered, however latently, by new versions of either Bossuet's optimism or Spengler's pessimism. Optimism and pessimism do not help us reach a true understanding of the plurality and ambiguity of our history.

Resistance, attention, and hope are more plausible strategies. We can, for example, continue the search of such great modernists as Eliade and Jung, Woolf and Faulkner, Stravinsky and Chagall for uncovering archetypes in our relationships with myth and with the cosmos itself. These modernist strategies challenge our Western obsession with finding all meaning in history alone. Alternatively, with postmodernist writers, filmmakers, and rock musicians, we can invent new antinarratives to evoke the chaos that is our historical situation. With the best interpreters of the ancient classics, we can also continue to risk a conversation with the astounding claims of all our founding texts. We can continue strategies like that of Georg Lukacs[25] by searching for the Utopian impulses hidden in the great realistic narratives of our recent past (Balzac, Dickens, Brontë, Melville). We should, above all, learn to listen to the narratives of others, especially those "others" who have had to suffer our otherness imposed upon their interpretations of their own history and classics. Through all these conflicting strategies, we should at least recognize that the de-centering of the Western ego can also occasion a de-centering of our Eurocentric history. And that resistance to ourselves is also hope.

We can rediscover this same kind of insight in the classics with a power that often shames our modern theories. Aeschylus and Sophocles, after all, are experts in ambiguity, Euripides in plurality. Isaiah and Jeremiah can teach some to resist with the fierceness demanded by the times. Job, Ruth, and Ecclesiastes can teach others what hope means in despairing times. Through interpretation we can enter into the startling metaphors of Sappho, the conversations of Plato's Socrates, the arguments of Aristotle, or the parables of Jesus.

Another strategy is to study any plausible modern critical theory of self and society that may clarify some of our suspicions. Indeed, if history itself is not to become a listing of random events ("one damn thing after another") or a form of entertainment for the intellectual classes, then modern critical analyses of the social sciences should also be used.[26] One need not become a Weberian pessimist to learn from his analyses of the rationalization and bureaucratization of all reality in modernity. One need not succumb to Marxist economism to learn from Marxist analyses of the material realities in all culture.[27] One need not endorse Lewis Mumford's technologism to learn how profoundly technological changes—including our present postindustrial technology—affect all history.[28]

Should these interruptions lead us to believe that something is fundamentally and systemically awry in our history and society? We can trust ourselves to conversation and argument when our only problem is error. But if we face something more elusive and profound than error, if we face systemic distortion, then another intellectual strategy is also called for. That other strategy we name a hermeneutics of suspicion.[29]

To understand the difference between an error and a systemic distortion is to understand a central difference between modernity and postmodernity. A modern consciousness is modern by pinning all its hopes on rational consciousness. From the first Socratic and Sophistic intellectual revolutions in Athens through the seventeenth-century scientific revolution, the eighteenth-century Enlightenment, and the various strategies of reason in the nineteenth and twentieth centuries, both classical reason and modern rationality have been propelled by an unconscious optimism. Only the mindless would want to rid our culture of the emancipatory discoveries of Western reason. But postmodern consciousness, which was first expressed in modernity by Nietzsche's struggle with the ambiguity in Socrates' belief in reason and then by Kierkegaard's exposure of the comic dilemma of the Hegelians, now deeply suspects the optimism concealed in Western notions of reason.

Rational consciousness is part of the best of our history: the cultural analyses of much traditional humanism; the methods of some historians of the history of ideas; the realistic and naturalist narratives of many novelists; the conceptual analyses of many modern philosophers; the model of enlightenment alive in many understandings of modernity; that same model, now disseminated widely, in much modern psychology.[30] In every case, an optimistic belief in the triumph of rational consciousness lives on. Error is, of course, a problem for that consciousness. Indeed error is the only problem for so optimistic an account of reason. For the autonomous, mature, coherent, modern self can surely handle error by finding better rational arguments or more reasonable conversation as it moves ineluctably forward into further enlightenment.

At their best, religions resist modernity by resisting sanguine versions of error, rational consciousness, and the self. For Christianity, for example, sin is not mere error. Sin is understood as inauthentic existence, at once a state of being and a personal responsibility. Sin posits itself. Sin pervades and de-centers the self's evasions, whether subtle or brutal. The self keeps turning in upon itself (*curvatus in se*) in an ever-subtler dialectic of self-delusion. This demand for the domination of all reality by means of an all-consuming self is not a mere error but something more pervasive and more fatal. It is named radical alienation or systemic distortion from the viewpoint of the self.[31] It is named sin from the viewpoint of Ultimate Reality: a perverse denial of one's finitude and a willful rejection of any dependence on Ultimate Reality. Through that denial, the self alienates itself as well from nature, history, others, and, in the end, from itself. This insistence on the inevitability of sin was too often accompanied, it is true, by intemperate attacks on all reason. Nevertheless, whether we name it sin or alienation, this systemic distortion cannot but be noticed by any reader of the great classics of Western Christianity, from Augustine through Luther, Calvin, Pascal, Kierkegaard and the great neoorthodox theologians of the early twentieth century.[32]

We can understand what a Christian means by sin, it is true, only by grasping what a Christian means by grace. For a radical Christian like Dostoyevsky in *The Brothers Karamazov,* you can have as radical a doctrine of sin as you wish as long as your doctrine of grace is equally radical. Indeed, as Kierkegaard's analysis of the dialectic of the self makes clear, we understand sin only by facing the power of God's grace. Grace comes as both gift and threat. As gift, grace can turn one completely around (*conversio*) into a transformed life of freedom. Yet grace also comes as threat by casting a harsh light upon what we have done to ourselves and our willingness to destroy any reality, even Ultimate Reality, if we cannot master it. Grace is a word Christians use to name this extraordinary process: a power erupting in one's life as a gift revealing that Ultimate Reality can be trusted as the God who is Pure, Unbounded Love; a power interrupting our constant temptations to delude ourselves at a level more fundamental than any conscious error; a power gradually but really transforming old habits.[33] No interpreter can understand what Christians mean without using the language of power: a power that comes as both gift and threat to judge and heal, not fundamentally moral transgressions or sins, not errors, not mistakes, but that ultimate systemic distortion, sin itself. This is what Ivan Karamazov understood but the Grand Inquisitor did not.

Other religions, especially the many forms of Buddhism, illustrate an analogous insight into the human condition by their teaching that ordinary consciousness is an illusion grounded in a primal ignorance (avidya).[34] Initially we merely suspect that we may suffer from illusion. Only through some journey of enlightenment to a higher consciousness and its disclosure of Ultimate Reality as emptiness or suchness do we rightly interpret the full extent of our most fundamental systemic illusion, that primal avidya that constantly tempts us to believe in the powers of both ordinary consciousness and rationality. Only then can we cease clinging to our most cherished illusion, the substantial self, by letting go to experience our radical relatedness to the cosmos. The gift of this enlightenment is inevitably a threat as well, as it attacks all our usual understandings of the self. With such enlightenment, the transformed self can finally realize that samsara and nirvana are one. At their best the religions remind any modern mind capable of risking an interpretation of the classic religious texts that all is not well with modern rational consciousness.[35] The modern ego is built on quicksand. Something more than mere error is at stake. Something sturdier than either optimism or pessimism is needed. Something may be more drastically awry than even Freud or Marx, with their differing analyses of our systemic distortions, suspected: sin and avidya.

The religions, however, also bear their own ambiguous history of effects, including the effects of the categories sin and avidya. Towards the end of this book we shall study more fully this return of the religions into the postmodern consciousness. At present, we may simply note that the religions have resources worthy of an effort to understand. Modernity, however, learned some of the lessons of the limitations of the model of rationality embodied in what Westerners continue to call *the* Enlightenment by turning to nonreligious, indeed often antireligious, mentors. The great "posttheologians" of secular culture—Darwin, Marx, Freud, Nietzsche, and the feminist thinkers—have taught through their otherwise conflicting narratives a single lesson: the fragile character of modern rational consciousness. And that fragility, in turn, has yielded a series of conflicting suspicions about the existence of unconscious systemic distortions—not mere conscious errors—in our individual and communal lives.

This lesson has been intensified by recent studies on the relationships of language and knowledge. All the posttheologians have been interpreted anew through studies of their language. Indeed, the developments in much of the most radical secular thought of our period are largely exercises in retrieving Nietzsche's radical rhetorization of "language," "reality," and "truth." For example, the leitmotiv of all the pluralistic strategies of deconstruction may be found in this classic text of Nietzsche:

What, then, is truth? A mobile army of metaphors, metonyms, and anthropomorphisms—in short, a sum of human relations, which have been enhanced, transposed, and embellished poetically and rhetorically, and which after long use seem firm, canonical, and obligatory to a people: truths are illusions about which one has forgotten that this is what they are: metaphors which are worn out and without sensuous power. . . .[36]

The terrifying otherness of an unconscious structured like a language, a language where the signifiers, not the signifieds,

reign, has reemerged to disclose and conceal a split in consciousness itself. From that split has emerged a series of ruptures in
the self that no mere argument or conversation can undo—not
even that strange anticonversation between analyst and analy-
sand culminating in the process of transference and counter-
transference. Freed from their scientism and economism, their
Leninist and Stalinist totalitarian readings, as well as sanguine
humanist readings, the texts of Marx have once again become
frightening revelations of what ideology, in the hard sense,
means.[37] Ideology is not confined to those conscious beliefs and
values familiar to all Zeitgeist analysts. Ideologies are unconscious but systemically functioning attitudes, values, and beliefs
produced by and in the material conditions of all uses of language, all analyses of truth, and all claims to knowledge.[38] More
than any others, feminist thinkers have demonstrated that language was never innocent—especially the phallocentric language
of "the man of reason."[39]

Suffering, however repressed, eventually erupts to subvert
our most basic modern belief: the belief that somehow we can
think our way through once more. The split self of postmodernity is caught between conscious activity and a growing realization of the radical otherness not only around but within us.
We name that otherness, after all, the unconscious, not the preconscious, or even the subconscious. Ideologies are carried in
and by the very language we use to know any reality at all. The
critique of ideologies insists that all interpretations of every culture and every classic should include an analysis of the material
conditions that underlie both its production and its reception.

Any postmodern position intensifies the central insight that
has guided us throughout these reflections: all experience and
all understanding is hermeneutical. To interpret well must now
mean that we attend to and use the hermeneutics of both retrieval and suspicion. The moderns were relatively untroubled
by reflection upon the indissoluble relationships between knowledge and language. They were relatively confident about the
power of reflection to eliminate error and render consciousness
translucent if not transparent. At the end of the day, despite all
its transcendental "turns to the subject," modern consciousness
remained a relatively stable and manageable affair.[40]

It seems oddly unimaginative that the only name we have

for our period is that vague and ambiguous expression "the post-modern." But there we are. The fact is we have left modernity behind.[41] We have left any belief in the transparency of consciousness to itself. Reality and knowledge are now linked to language. And with a heightened sense of language, the interruptive realities of history and society have entered consciousness anew.[42]

Postmodernity demands multiple discourses for interpretation itself. As postmodern writers and thinkers remind us, we live within intertextuality.[43] Texts and methods of interpretation often conflict. They may even attempt to annihilate one another. Texts sometimes complete one another in the manner of a Hegelian *Aufhebung*. Methods sometimes complement one another. As that sense of intertextuality increases, what shall we say? No text is an island complete unto itself? Should we now anticipate the almost inevitable arrival of a new antinovel entitled *A Farewell to Texts*? We have, after all, already received a volume from a major critic entitled *Is There A Text in This Class?*[44]

We begin to suspect that consciousness itself is radically intertextual. Perhaps it only seems this way because we will not face the dispossession of the ego by all the plural and ambiguous texts that have usurped its will to domination disguised as the self's will to truth.[45] Reason can be so driven by a debilitating optimism that it will not dwell for long upon either the radical interruptions of history or the unconscious distortions of self and culture. It is not merely that reason will not sometimes stay for an answer, but that it will not even wait for a question.

No less than Plato, our hope too is grounded in conversation. But before we presume to participate in that hope, we need to face the repressed complicity that every notion of participation now cannot but suggest. Otherness has entered, and it is no longer outside us among the "others." The most radical otherness is within. Unless we acknowledge that, it will be impossible for us to responsibly participate in, or meaningfully belong to, our history.

The return of the same can now be understood as what it always was: a return to policies of exclusion and repression. What sameness remains is caught in the web of otherness and indeterminacy. What similarity is possible must now occur as similarity-in-difference. We can trust ourselves to a conversation with the classics with this proviso: we admit that everything—ourselves, our texts, and the conversation itself—is deeply affected by the ambiguity and plurality that touch all. Retrieval now demands both critique and suspicion. Indeed, retrieval can now often come best through critique and suspicion. And even when retrieval enters on its own, it can no longer arrive unambiguously. There is no innocent interpretation, no innocent interpreter, no innocent text.

Consider, for example, Michel Foucault's analyses of different discourses in our history:[46] the discourses of penology, medicine, law, sexuality, madness, and reason, indeed the discourse on discourse itself in the modern development of disciplines and specializations. What these analyses show is that every discourse bears within itself the anonymous and repressed actuality of highly particular arrangements of power and knowledge. Every discourse, by operating under certain assumptions, necessarily excludes other assumptions. Above all, our discourses exclude those others who might disrupt the established hierarchies or challenge the prevailing hegemony of power.

And yet the voices of the others multiply:[47] the hysterics and mystics speaking through Lacan; the mad and the criminals allowed to speak by Foucault; the primal peoples, once misnamed the primitives, defended and interpreted by Eliade; the dead whose story the victors still presume to tell; the repressed suffering of peoples cheated of their own experience by modern mass media; the poor, the oppressed, and the marginalized—all those considered "nonpersons" by the powerful but declared by the great prophets to be God's own privileged ones. All the victims of our discourses and our history have begun to discover their own discourses in ways that our discourse finds difficult to hear, much less listen to. Their voices can seem strident and uncivil—in a word, other. And they are. We have all just begun to sense the terror of that otherness. But only by beginning to listen to those other voices may we also begin to hear the otherness within our own discourse and within ourselves. What we might then begin to hear, above our own chatter, are possibilities we have never dared to dream.

Are there any arguments appropriate for analyzing the interruptions that postmodern suspicion has cast upon conversation? They would have to be able not only to remedy the errors we are used to analyzing through more familiar kinds of argument, but also to spot and, if possible, alleviate the systemic distortions we have begun to suspect do exist.[48] Even arguments in postmodernity prove peculiar. They are called "critical theories."[49] Any critical theory is a fragile but essential tool that can and should be used. Any theory is fragile insofar as it is affected by the pluralistic and ambiguous reality of all discourse. Any theorist is tempted to make her or his theory the one innocent, free, noncontextual hope for emancipation and enlightenment. The slide from a once-emancipatory critical theory to hardened dogma or domesticated truism affects all theories and all discourse—as the history of Marxist societies demonstrates; as the domestication of Freud by our psychological culture shows; as the political resurgence of social Darwinism, that travesty of Darwin, more than suggests. And yet critical theories like psychoanalytic theory and the critique of ideology remain useful modes of argument in our period.

Any theory that allows primacy to critical reflection is on the way to becoming critical theory. A critical theory in the full sense, however, is any theory that renders explicit how cognitive reflection can throw light on systemic distortions, whether individual or social, and through that illumination allow some emancipatory action. Reason, on this model, serves the interest of both enlightenment and emancipation. The peculiarity of critical theories is really not these aims, which are, after all, the aims of Aristotle's rhetoric, ethics, and politics. The uniqueness of modern critical theories—like those of the Frankfurt school—is that our situation is now acknowledged to be far more historically conditioned, pluralistic, and ambiguous than theories like Aristotle's could acknowledge.[50]

Whether those theories are labeled critical theories or are called by some other name matters little. Any enlightenment that critical theory can provide is necessarily partial—as the best critical theorists, like Adorno, insisted.[51] Any emancipation is inevitably limited—as feminist theorists made clear. Aristotle's phronesis retains its remarkable interpretive power, but linked as it now must be to critical theory, it becomes a genuinely new strategy of attention, resistance, and hope.[52]

The twentieth century's interpretation of language and history has proved an unnerving journey: from the endless number of language games in Wittgenstein, through the otherness of the play of the signifiers in every signified, to the discovery that our discourse is not only dispersed but bears within itself the whole ambiguous history of the effects of power. This history of effects can work silently but no less effectively to exclude everything except what goes without saying. We may continue to try to persuade ourselves of our autonomy, our innocence, and our idealism. Our theories can become exercises in passive contemplation of mere possibilities, or deceptively hard exercises excluding anything not fitting an already determined model. Our theories and our conversations can become, however, what they in fact always were: limited, fragile, necessary exercises in reaching relatively adequate knowledge of language and history alike.

In one sense, this entire journey has brought us back to where we began: reflecting on the beginnings of modernity in that palimpsest of events, symbols, texts, movements, and persons we must now hesitantly name the French Revolution. We have not resolved our original puzzlement, how to interpret that event. And yet, perhaps through that very return, we can now know that we do not know that place—our place—for the first time.

CHAPTER 5

Resistance and Hope: The Question of Religion

The purely autonomous ego was mortally wounded when it was found that if language was not its instrument, then the subject was no longer in control. Furthermore, radical plurality and ambiguity have undermined its once-assertive claims to mastery and domination.

And yet I write this book, and you read it. How? Who are the "I" writing and the "I" reading? The self cannot be that solitary freedom tinged with despair of the existentialists, or the autonomous self of the Enlightenment, or the expressive self of the romantics, or the pretense at no-self of the positivists. The self is somewhere else. But where? Perhaps experiencing the pleasures of irony in the abyss of indeterminacy? Perhaps trapped in the interstices of all the historical institutions and discourses that formed the modern self in the first place? But now, through the new discourse on discourse itself, are we finally witnessing the erasure of this figure in the sand?[1]

It is indeed true that for postmodernity the purely autonomous ego is no more. And yet the subject, however chastened and transformed, has not been erased.[2] As subjects we can resist our former illusions of pure autonomy by risking interpretations of all the classic signs and texts. The postmodern subject now knows that any route to reality must pass through the radical plurality of our differential languages and the ambiguity of all our histories. After such knowledge, what identity, what coherence, for what self? The coherent self attempted by the realistic and naturalist narrators of coherence is gone, to be replaced by a more fragile self—open to epiphanies—as we find in Joyce, Proust, and Woolf. We may still experience moments of true manifestation in our conversation with classics. But even these moments of recognition come to us now not as returns of the same but as unsettling acknowledgements of the other and the different become, at their best, the possible as the analogous.

In postmodernity, resistance may take the form of a breaking of all the codes of traditional narratives in order to allow language and history to disrupt the self of the reader. Resistance may be Nietzsche's joyous affirmation of plurality itself, alive again in the unstable ironies of Barthes, de Man, and Derrida, alive as well in the encyclopedias become labyrinths of Borges. Resistance also may take the form of Foucault's "dry-as-dust" archival research on the institutions and almost impenetrable codes of power and knowledge in all historical and scientific discourses.

Postmodern acts of resistance are, to be sure, often acts of resistance against their own intent: de Man resisting the political implications of his work, Nabokov rejecting all searches for symbols in the reflective surfaces of his chessboard texts, Cioran's fall into time, Beckett abandoning hope as illusion, and Foucault's reluctance to endorse the power of resistance in his own analyses. And yet, despite themselves, all the postmoderns can give us, if not some *promesse de bonheur*, at least the promise of whatever hope has empowered the acts of resistance that are their writings.

Any intellectual resistance in our period must go through, not the "fiery brook" of Feuerbach's traditional humanism, but the labyrinth revealed by contemporary encyclopedias of multidisciplinary knowledge. Any retrieval of the classics currently available is likely to be the result of deep suspicion. Postmodern coherence, at best, will be a rough coherence: interrupted, obscure, often confused, self-conscious of its own language use and, above all, aware of the ambiguities of all histories and traditions.

If the religions enter into this scene of conflict, they must be able to resist the illusory models of pure autonomy and easy coherence. Despite their own sin and ignorance, the religions, at their best, always bear extraordinary powers of resistance. When not domesticated as sacred canopies for the status quo[3] nor wasted by their own self-contradictory grasps at power, the religions live by resisting. The chief resistance of religions is to more of the same. Through their knowledge of sin and ignorance, the religions can resist all refusals to face the radical plurality and ambiguity of any tradition, including their own.[4] Through their most fundamental beliefs in Ultimate Reality, the religions can resist the ego's compulsive refusal to face the always already power of that Ultimate Reality that bears down upon us.[5] The religions also resist the temptations of many postmodernists to see the problem but not to act. But the religions also join secular postmodernity in resisting all earlier modern, liberal, or neoconservative contentment with the ordinary discourse on rationality and the self.

Above all, the religions are exercises in resistance. Whether seen as Utopian visions or believed in as revelations of Ultimate Reality, the religions reveal various possibilities for human freedom that are not intended for that curious distancing act that has become second nature to our aesthetic sensibilities.[6] Neither Zen Buddhism nor Yoga, for example, should be reduced to sets of techniques designed to provide new realms of pleasure for the restless self.[7] Zen is a spiritual exercise that uses its extraordinary set of techniques to train both body and mind to a vision of what reality is not ("what goes without saying") and what reality ultimately is ("suchness," "emptiness").

To interpret the religious classics is to allow them to challenge what we presently consider possible. To interpret them is also to allow ourselves to challenge them through every hermeneutic of critique, retrieval, and suspicion we possess. To understand them at all we must converse with them. But no more than with any other classics do we converse with them if we only passively contemplate their suggestiveness. If we would understand the religions at all, we must allow for a genuine conversation with them on the meaning and truth of their classics and the applicability or nonapplicability of their strategies of resistance.

Theological interpretation is one way to allow that genuine conversation with the religious classics.[8] As reflection on Ultimate Reality, and thereby on the limit questions of our existence, theological interpretation, like all such interpretations, must always be a highly precarious mode of inquiry.[9] Theologians can never claim certainty but, at best, highly tentative relative adequacy. Theologians cannot escape the same plurality and ambiguity that affect all discourse. Theologians attempt to envision some believable hope by testing critically all religious claims to ultimate hope. As the careers of Mahatma Gandhi and Martin Luther King, Jr., show, theologians, at their best, can help us all discover new modes of action that are, ethically, politically, and religiously, acts of resistance to the status quo. They believe that hope is granted by the one Reality that, as Ultimate, must be radically other and different, however that Reality is named—Emptiness, the One, God, Suchness.[10]

And yet many postmoderns resist these controversial interpretations of religion called theologies. Their reasons vary greatly. Some do not want to think any longer about theology, for the religions seem to be spent forces. Some may want, with Richard Rorty—here an elegant spokesperson for the leisured classes—simply "to change the subject."[11] For others, the religions are quickly dismissed through some unspoken combination of unhappy childhood memories of religion and secretly Whig histories of Western progress.[12] For yet others, both theologies and even the religions they interpret may seem trapped in onto-theo-logical or purely idealist discourse.[13] Still others—and this, I believe, is the most serious charge—find themselves, despite their acknowledgement of the cultural and ethical achievements of religion, unable to consider seriously the intellectual claims of theology because the history of religions also includes such an appalling litany of murder, inquisitions, holy wars, obscurantisms, and exclusivisms.

There is every good reason to take these ethical charges seriously. Any religion, whether past or present, in a position of power surely demonstrates that religious movements, like secular ones, are open to corruption. The impacted memories of religious fanaticism and its demonic history of effects upon all cultures are memories that cannot be erased. Whoever comes to speak in favor of religion and its possibilities of enlightenment and emancipation does not come with clean hands nor with a clear conscience. If interpreters of religion come with any pretense to purity, they should not be listened to. If religious thinkers will not combat the obscurantisms, exclusivisms, and moral fanaticisms within their own religious tradition, how can the rest of us take them seriously as providing new strategies of resistance?[15] The Metternich policy of too many religious leaders—liberalism abroad but suppression within the empire—deserves the contempt of the religious and the nonreligious alike. As Pascal, surely no stranger to the possibilities of faith, once insisted, "Men never do evil so completely and cheerfully as when they do it from religious conviction."[16]

There are, therefore, many good reasons to pause before entering to speak on behalf of interpreting the religious classics. The religions, in fact, are even more intensely pluralistic and ambiguous than art, morality, philosophy, and politics. Given the nature of the subject matter of religion, this is necessarily the case. For religions do claim, after all, that Ultimate Reality has revealed itself and that there is a way of liberation for any human being. But even this startling possibility can only be understood by us if we will risk interpreting it. It is possible that some interpreters may have encountered the power of Ultimate Reality. They may have experienced, therefore, religious enlightenment and emancipation. But these claims can be interpreted only by the same kinds of human beings as before: finite and contingent members of particular societies and cultures. They demand our best efforts at rigorous, critical, and genuine conversation. They demand retrieval, critique, and suspicion.

Any human being can interpret the religious classics because any human being can ask the fundamental questions that are part of the very attempt to become human at all, those questions that the religious classics address. Among the fundamental questions are those peculiar questions named religious or limit questions: questions provoked by radical contingency and mortality; questions evoked by the transience of all things human; questions attendant upon an acknowledgment of the historical and social contingency of all the values embraced and all the convictions lived by; the question of suffering, that contrast experience par excellence, which enters every life at some point to interrupt its continuities and challenge its seeming security; the question of the meaning of that ennui that can erupt into a pervasive anxiety, even terror, in the face of some unnameable other that seems to bear down upon us at certain moments; the question of why we sense some responsibility to live an ethical life even when we cannot rationally prove why we should be ethical at all; the question of why we might need to affirm a belief that there is some fundamental order in reality that allows scientific inquiry; the question of the possible nature of that order revealed in the new physics and the new astronomies and cosmologies; the question of how to understand the oppression endured by so many of the living as well as the subversive memories of the suffering of the dead alive in the narratives, sagas, and folktales of every people; the question of how to face the alienation lurking in all irony; the question of the need to understand what possible meaning might be present in the profound love and joy we experience; the question of why I possess a fundamental trust that both allows me to go on at all and is not reducible to all my other trusts; the question of why an occasional sense, however transient, of the sheer giftedness of reality can be experienced when I finally stop clinging and sense the truth in Wittgenstein's statement "That the world is, is the mystical"; the question of whether I too experience moments that bear some family resemblance to those "consolations without a cause" of which the mystics wrote; the questions evoked by the postmodern sense that I have, at best, a "learned ignorance" of what it means to be a human being; the question of why even that learned ignorance seems to betray a more primal ignorance whose contours I may glimpse in the play of the signifiers in all my language and knowledge, as well as the play of that pluralistic and ambiguous history to which I belong far more than either language or history can possibly belong to me; the questions provoked by the sense that in every act of resistance some strange and unnameable hope, however inchoate, betrays itself.

Like strictly metaphysical questions, the fundamental questions of religion must be logically odd questions, since they are questions about the most fundamental presuppositions, the most basic beliefs, of all our knowing, willing, and acting.[17] Like strictly metaphysical questions, religious questions must be questions on the nature of Ultimate Reality. Unlike metaphysical questions, religious questions deliberately ask the question of the meaning and truth of Ultimate Reality not only as it is in itself but as it is existentially related to us. The religious classics are testimonies to the responses of the religions to those questions.[18] They are testimonies by human beings who, like ourselves, have asked these questions and believe that they have received a response from Ultimate Reality itself. They believe, therefore, that some revelation has occurred giving them a new possibility of enlightenment or even some new way to formulate the question. They believe in following some way of religious liberation by which they may become related to all reality through a trusting relationship to that Ultimate Reality that as ultimate is the origin and end of all. If, in the course of any interpretation of any religious classic, other intepreters find that the language of belief is not persuasive, they can still develop their own responses to these logically odd religious questions. Any interpreter who is willing to ask the fundamental questions to which the religious classics respond can and should converse with them.

Not only religious believers, therefore, should risk interpretations of the religious classics. Some interpret the religious classics not as testimonies to a revelation from Ultimate Reality, as religious believers will, of course, interpret them, but as testimonies to possibility itself. As Ernst Bloch's interpretations of all those daydreams and Utopian and eschatological visions that Westerners have ever dared to dream argue, the religious classics can also become for nonbelieving interpreters testimonies to resistance and hope.[19] As Mircea Eliade's interpretations of the power of the archaic religions show, the historian of religions can help create a new humanism which retrieves forgotten religious classic symbols, rituals, and myths.[20] The great historians of religion show us how those primal memories live on in camouflaged forms. For those who doubt this, let them attend a single rock concert—an explosive expression of the power of the primal still alive in our day. Any reminder of our archaic roots by interpreters of ancient symbols, rites, and myths becomes an act of resistance—as anyone can acknowledge who observes that even sex, that last stronghold of the primal, can be forced to succumb to the techniques and knowledge of that modern Western invention, "sexuality."[21] These repressed memories can destroy the narrowness of our sense of possibility. They can entice us to hope for some other and different, yet possible, ways of thinking and empower our resistance. If the work of Bloch and Benjamin on the classic texts and symbols of the eschatological religions and the work of Eliade and others on the primal religions were allowed to enter into the contemporary conversation, then the range of possibilities we ordinarily afford ourselves would be exponentially expanded beyond reigning Epicurean, Stoic, and nihilistic visions.

Bloch's interpretation of the Utopian impulses of the religions is a significant contribution to postmodern thought. Believers, too, have learned from those interpretations. The believer's difference from interpretations of religion like Bloch's usually takes the form of a "Yes, but . . ."—as when a theologian like Metz, after acknowledging his debt to Bloch, will then add, "But we do not pray to Utopias." The implication of that "but" is clear: When a Jew, a Christian, or a Muslim says the word *God*, he or she means the Ultimate Reality from which all comes and toward which all moves. Believers mean by God not a product of their creative imaginations but the one to whom they pray—the Ultimate Reality, the origin and end of all reality. For believers, to be enlightened religiously is to be empowered to understand: to understand, above all, a power that is the ultimate power with which we all must deal.[22]

Through that religious understanding, we may also come to sense the pluralistic and ambiguous reality of the self, at once finite, estranged, and needing of liberation by a power not its own. There are many models of religious enlightenment, sometimes complementary, more often conflicting: a radical enlightenment to emptiness as the Ultimate Reality in many of the Buddhist ways; an enlightenment to "That art Thou" (Atman and Brahman are one) in much of Hinduism; an elightenment to a compassion so great that we become willing to postpone our own final enlightenment to work for that of others in the Bodhisattva traditions of Buddhism; an enlightenment to a sense of our precarious but necessary relations to the whole through the civic order in the civil religions of the Greeks, the Romans, and the Confucians; an enlightenment to our relations to all living things in Taoism and in the primal, archaic religions; an enlightenment to God's law as delineating the way in Judaism; an enlightenment to a life oriented by radical faith, hope, and love in Christianity; an enlightenment to political and historical responsibility in the prophetic strands of Judaism, Christianity, and Islam. Despite their often radical differences, as John Hick suggests,[23] all these ways do demand a singular transformation of the self: from self-centeredness to Reality-centeredness. In any religious way, we must shift our center from the ego, by means of that new relationship with Ultimate Reality. Only then can the self cease to be an ego and find some authentic freedom by being related to nature, history, others, and even the now transformed self. It is implausible, of course, that all these religious enlightenments are, in any meaningful sense, different expressions of the same religious position. The plurality among the religions is not reducible to claims that they all bespeak the same enlightenment or practice the same way of liberation.

There are family resemblances among the religions. But as far as I can see, there is no single essence, no one content of enlightenment or revelation, no one way of emancipation or liberation, to be found in all that plurality. There are different construals of the nature of Ultimate Reality itself: God, Emptiness, Suchness, the One, Nature, the Many. There are different understandings of what has been revealed by Ultimate Reality about Ultimate Reality and thereby about ourselves in our relationships of harmony and disharmony with that reality. Granted these differences, there are different interpretations of what way we should follow to move from a fatal self-centeredness to a liberating Reality-centeredness. The discourses and ways of the religions can sometimes complement or even, at the limit, complete some undeveloped aspect of one another. The religions can also interrupt and, at the other limit, obliterate one another's claims. There is no way to tell before the conversation which option is the right one. To want more is to try to be freed from the demands of interpretation.

Pluralism—more accurately, perhaps, a pluralistic attitude—is one possible response to the fact of religious plurality. It is an attitude I fundamentally trust. But whenever any affirmation of pluralism, including my own, past and present, becomes simply a passive response to more and more possibilities, none of which shall ever be practiced, then pluralism demands suspicion. That kind is, as Simone de Beauvoir insisted, the perfect ideology for the modern bourgeois mind. Such a pluralism masks a genial confusion in which one tries to enjoy the pleasures of difference without ever committing oneself to any particular vision of resistance and hope.

The great pluralists in the history of Western thought—especially that still too neglected thinker, William James—knew that any worthy affirmation of plurality was the beginning, but never the end, of a responsibly pluralistic attitude.[24] There must be other criteria besides those of possibility and openness. There must be criteria to assess the coherence or incoherence of any possibility with what we otherwise know or, more likely, believe to be the case. There must be ethical-political criteria on what the religious option will mean for both individual and society. James's generosity of temperament flourished at times into an exhilaration in the "blooming, buzzing confusion" of experience itself. That Jamesian joy was real, but it was never his whole message. James's pragmatic theory of truth had problems, but the problem was never his insistence on the need for a pragmatic assessment of all discourse on truth. A pragmatic moment, as contemporary discourse analysis shows, is present whether we acknowledge it or not.

The break with the spectator view of knowledge by the classic pragmatists has been their singular contribution to contemporary discussions of reasonable criteria for assessment. They taught us to focus on possibilities and thereby on the future. They instructed us on how to assess the coherence or incoherence of all claims by judging them in relationship to the most relatively adequate consensual knowledge we possess.[25] They helped us understand the modern need to assess the ethical fruits (James) and the social-political consequences (Dewey) of all possibilities.

The plurality of interpretations of religion is a fact, as is the resulting conflict of interpretations. The great pluralists of religion are those who so affirm plurality that they fundamentally trust it, yet do not shirk their responsibility to develop criteria of assessment for each judgment of relative adequacy. This does not mean, however, that only the pluralistic interpreters of religion should be heeded. Quite the contrary: if a pluralistic attitude is genuine, it will be willing to learn from anyone—including, and sometimes especially, the great monistic interpreters of religion. Does anyone really wish that Luther, instead of simply stating, "Here I stand; I can do no other," had added *sotto voce*, "But if it really bothers you, I will move"?[26] Any pluralist who cannot learn from Luther's classic interpretation of Christianity can hardly learn from any interpretation of religion at all. Even the pluralist—usually more tentatively but no less firmly—must one day speak her or his "Here I stand" or prove unfaithful to the demands for critical assessment.

The plurality of interpretations of religion is more than equaled by the plurality of the religions themselves. The belief that ultimately all the religious are finally one is implausible. Even mystical traditions are as plural in their aims, techniques, practices, and discourse as all other religious phenomena. The attempt to define a single "perennial philosophy" grounding all the religions, whether expressed impressionistically by Aldous Huxley or rigorously by Henry Corbin, Fritz Schuon, and Huston Smith, is a commendable experiment but thus far not a persuasive one. Mystical experience, like all other experience, is also interpretation, and, like all other interpretation, mysticism participates in the discourse of highly particular traditions and societies. The claim that Narganjuna and Eckhart are experiencing or interpreting the same reality appears implausible. That there are profound similarities between them is obvious, but those similarities are at best analogies, that is, similarities-in-difference.

Even the similarity in the limit questions of the religions is not identity. For example, the metaphors of depth usually employed in Western language for religious questions—the "ultimate concern" language of Tillich, the dialectical language of intensification in Kierkegaard, or even my own language of limit questions—are similar to, but also notably different from, the surface metaphors used by Chan and Zen Buddhist questioners.[27] The responses of the religions, their various narratives, doctrines, and symbols, and their often conflicting accounts of the way to authentic liberation are at least as different as they are similar. They are clearly not the same.

There are many ways to be religious. No single definition of what religion is can master that variety. Perhaps even the word religion itself, with its Western overtones, should be abandoned in favor of an expression like "ways to Ultimate Reality."[28] Conversation is not only possible among the religions; conversation is now a necessity. But a conversation that assumes, prior to the conversation itself, that all the religions are really the same can hardly help. There are few more important conversations than the dialogues among the great religions, and few more difficult ones.[29] If those conversations are to be fruitful, all conversation partners should keep in mind the full complexity of the process of interpretation itself. Otherwise they may find themselves with one more candidate for a definition of religion whose lowest common denominator status will satisfy no one.

A strategy for this difficult dialogue I have earlier named "an analogical imagination." As a heuristic and pluralistic strategy, it may also prove useful for the conversation among the religions. The phrase can remind conversation partners that difference and otherness once interpreted *as* other and *as* different are thereby acknowledged as in some way possible and, in the end, analogous.[30] Any one who can converse can learn to appropriate another possibility. Between person and person, as well as between person and text, there exists in every authentic conversation an openness to mutual transformation.[31] But any interpretation of some "other" is my appropriation of a possibility that is no longer exactly the same as it was in the original form. No Westerner, for example, can "turn East" except as a Westerner who has turned East.[32] As the development of new forms of Buddhism in the West, especially in North America, demonstrates, when Buddhism becomes a religious option for Westerners, the traditional ways of Buddhism in Eastern cultures are changed by this new journey to the West.[33] Western ways of being Buddhist are as different from all earlier ones as they are from one another: Indian, Tibetan, Southeast Asian, Chinese, and Japanese. Since there are sufficient family resemblances among the many ways, it is possible to describe them all as Buddhist. Within any great religious way there exist many options.

What we are likely to find in any conversation that does not repress plurality by fiat are, at best, analogies. Analogical language was the creation of Aristotle, that sometime pluralist,[34] to find an alternative langauge besides the usual candidates: a univocal language where all is the same and an equivocal language where all is different. Authentic analogical language is a rare achievement, since it attempts the nearly impossible: an articulation of real differences as genuinely different but also similar to what we already know.[35] On a more existential level, an analogical imagination suggests a willingness to enter the conversation, that unnerving place where one is willing to risk all one's present self-understanding by facing the claims to attention of the other.[36] In any conversation we may find ourselves called to change either radically, as suggested by the religious language

of conversion, or less completely but genuinely, as in any acknowledgment of the once merely different as now genuinely
possible.

Christians, for example, can convert to Buddhism and vice
versa. Alternatively, Christians can so learn from Zen that they,
like Thomas Merton, though not converting, do become what
might be described as self-transcending Christians, even Zen
Christians.[37] The profound Buddhist insight into the self's need
to stop its compulsive clinging to all false securities has caused
some Christian theologians to realize that even the most refined
concepts of theism can function as fatal evasions of Ultimate
Reality. Indeed, the Buddhist-Christian dialogue has led some
Christian theologians to rethink much traditional Christian God-
language, as when they rediscover the power of Paul's "self-
emptying" language for Christ's salvific role or they appropriate
the once-puzzling language of Meister Eckhart on the "God-be-
yond-God."[38]

Some Buddhist appropriations of aspects of the Christian way
show the same kind of internal transformation as a result of a
genuine dialogue. Pauline self-emptying langauge has helped
some Zen Buddhists reinterpret one way that Ultimate Reality
as "Emptiness" is related to us.[39] Christian notions of grace as
gift have helped some Pure Land Buddhists to clarify their differences from other Buddhist traditions. Christian insistence that
the struggle for social justice is demanded by the command to
love has influenced some Buddhists in their reinterpretation to
include a concept of justice within the Buddhist call for compassion. Those new interpretations, in turn, have influenced
some revisionary Buddhist notions of karma.

The same analogical strategy may also assist interpreters to
reflect on plurality not only among the religions but within each
religion.[40] Our substantialist language again betrays us when we
use such words as *Judaism, Hinduism, Islam, Buddhism, Christianity.*
Although there are real family resemblances among the different
ways of being Jewish, Buddhist, or Muslim, these familiar nouns
are at best shorthand descriptions of each religious family. We
can sometimes trace the family resemblances or similarities-in-
difference in particular families: as historians of such well-doc-
umented families as the Tudors or the Stuarts, the Bourbons or
the Hapsburgs have. But as the history of any family shows, the

differences between, for example, Louis XIV and Louis XVI or between Maria Theresa and Joseph II are at least as significant as the similarities. Louis XIV and Louis XVI were, of course, not just genealogically but also, in some of their most characteristic actions, recognizably members of the same family. But the differences between them were sharp: they were different in temperament, character, and ways of thinking and acting. Suggestions as to how Louis XIV would have acted if he were his great-great-great-grandson facing a revolution seem irrelevant. Suggestions that Louis XVI could have domesticated an unruly bourgeoisie by luring them to Louis XIV's Versailles, that deconstructionist chamber of mirrors and manners, are bizarre at best.

Differences are too pronounced within a single family to try to explain them away by reducing them to simple variations on a single theme. As Ernst Troeltsch insisted, any attempt by Christians to formulate the essence of Christianity will prove to be a complex matter of critical interpretations, historical judgments, and ethical and religious decisions.[41] There are, to be sure, better and worse interpretations of any religion. The better interpretations are guided, I believe, by the kind of critical and necessarily general and flexible criteria set forth by Troeltsch in his classical essay "What Does 'Essence of Christianity' Mean?" As Isaiah Berlin once observed, any good pluralist should always be able to discuss the differences between good, bad, and downright awful interpretations. But there are no noninterpretive, ahistorical essences to be found in words like *Christianity*, *Judaism*, *Islam*, *Buddhism*, or *Hinduism*. Within each of these great ways and among the many similarities that render them distinct families, there remain many ways to be Christian, Jewish, Muslim, Buddhist, or Hindu.

In the light of the worldwide neoconservative resurgence, an insistence on the plurality of ways within every great religion is an ethical and religious responsibility. No thunderings from the Ayatollah Khomeini to his fellow Muslims, no peremptory decrees from the "Holy Office" to Roman Catholics, no threats from Reverend Falwell to his fellow Protestants, and no terror tactics by Rabbi Kehane directed at his fellow Jews should be allowed to destroy such an insistence.

No religious tradition, to my knowledge, has been as aware

of the ethical and religious need for affirming an internal plurality as has that manifold way we too easily call Hinduism. There is no religious classic as eloquent as the Bhagavad Gita in describing the religious importance of allowing many ways: the ways of knowledge, devotion, and action. Hinduism, with all its difficulties and all the necessary critiques and suspicions insisted upon by modern Hindus themselves, seems exemplary in its sense of the need for a genuine plurality within a common religious way.[42]

The other great religions, often less explicitly but no less forcefully, testify to the same religious need for a plurality of ways. To observe the history of any religion is to read a narrative of often radical plurality. To attack that plurality is to undermine some central religious power in the religion itself. For example, within the many possibilities within any great religious way, there is perhaps no option more important for the intellectuals in that religion to reflect upon than the ordinary ways practiced by most members of the religion. It should be humbling to realize that even if one's own interests are in the extraordinary expressions of the religion—the mystics, the prophets, the saints, the classics—this will not suffice for interpreting or practicing any religion. In one sense, of course, the interest in the intense forms of religion is a defensible option, since, as William James insisted, the intense instances are the clearest examples of religion as religion.[43] My own concern has, it must be admitted, the same Jamesian tone.

But even here, fresh critique and suspicion are needed. From the viewpoint of critique, the religions are carried along at least as much by the vast undertow of ordinary people leading ordinary religious lives as by the classic prophets, mystics, and saints. From the viewpoint of suspicion, our seeming inability to respond to other than classic examples is a clearly ambiguous phenomenon. If pluralists genuinely affirm plurality, they can hardly ignore, much less dismiss, the importance of ordinary and everyday examples of living a religious life.[44]

Latin American liberation theologians, for example, are clearly committed to an intense, prophetic reading of Christianity. Yet they have learned to pull back from their earlier rigorous criticisms of "popular religion": fatalism, mere blessing of the status quo, and dolorism.[45] They have learned to discern what these too easily dismissed popular expressions of religion might have to teach even the prophetic elite. My own theology of religious classics, as a second example, needs to suspect its predilection for extremities and intensifications.[46] It needs to learn better ways to be challenged by those other less obvious, only because less intense, classics—the ordinary practices, beliefs, and everyday rituals of all religious persons. Indeed, this is also true of the everyday lives of the intense ones; as the great exponent of extremity, Søren Kierkegaard, once remarked, interpreters can build castles with their thoughts, but like everyone else they live next door in a hut. If religious plurality is really to be honored, then no exponent of religious intensifications can ignore the classics of ordinary religious life in all the great ways: the bhakti traditions of Hinduism, the law's extraordinary attention to the details of everyday life in Judaism, the rituals and practices of ordinary nonenlightened Buddhists and nonsaintly Christians, the thrice-daily prayers and rituals of ordinary Muslims.

Theologians should not pretend that they understand any religion without interpreting it with the full demands we have seen that word to impose on all interpretations. Nor should they hope that such understanding-as-interpretation will be free from their own finitude, contingency, and faults. Karl Barth spoke for all theologians in all traditions when he stated, "The angels will laugh when they read my theology." Nor should theologians expect to be free of the unconscious systemic distortions that inevitably pervade all discourse. As Reinhold Niebuhr insisted, our best acts of creation are, at the same time, the best examples of our ambiguity. In principle, theologians should be open to every hermeneutic that can illuminate their demanding task. At their best, they are alert to any hermeneutic of retrieval that can interpret the religious event rightly, whether that event be the higher consciousness promoted and practiced in Yoga, in Zen, and in all the great mystical traditions or the gift and power of God's judgment and healing proclaimed in Judaism, Christianity, and Islam. Theologians should be alert as well to the need for any hermeneutic of suspicion that can further instruct their own religious suspicions of the endemic, unconscious reality of either sin, avidya, or dishonor. They should be open to any explanatory method—historical-critical methods, social-scientific methods, semiotic and structuralist methods, poststructuralist methods, hermeneutical discourse analysis—that can help to assess errors in traditional religious interpretations. They should use any form of argument that enhances the critical conversation with the classic religious texts and symbols. They should be open to any form of critical theory that helps spot the distortions suspected in the religious classics themselves.

Theological interpretations of the religions will, at best, be relatively adequate. Only a full conversation among all interpreters of religion, faithful to the demands of interpretation and cognizant of the multiple conflicts of interpretation on both religion and on interpretation, is likely to reach anything like a responsible consensus.[47] But even before such a consensus emerges, this much is clear: All interpreters of religion, whether believers or nonbelievers, can employ something like the theologian's sixth sense that to interpret religion at all demands being willing to put at risk one's present self-understanding in order to converse with the claim to attention of the religious classic. That instinctive sense is not only theologically but also hermeneutically sound. Like the classics of art and morality, the religious classics demand that we pay critical attention to their claims to truth if we are to understand their meaning at all.[48]

Hermeneutically, I am clearly not bound to either accept or reject any religious claims prior to the conversation itself. But if I would understand that claim, I am bound to struggle critically with the fact that its claim to truth is part of its meaning. To understand the religious classic at all, I cannot ultimately avoid its provocations to my present notions of what constitutes truth. The religious classic may be simply using another language to speak a truth I already know. If so, I should show how this is the case. The religious classic may be manifesting some reality different and other—even terrifyingly different and alienatingly other—from what I usually believe. If so, I should make clear how I understand the otherness and difference in this manifestation: Is it mad? impossible? possible? analogical? implausible? plausible? What might a mystical experience like Meister Eckhart's be like? And what might it mean for my present notions of possibility and truth? What might the higher consciousness of Zen be like? What can it mean for an interpreter who has never experienced it, yet senses some meaningfulness in its claim?

The claim to attention of any religious classic may either challenge or further confirm what I already know or believe to be true—or possibly true. Which is it? Why? Without asking these questions and attempting some reflective response, we are not fully interpreting even the meaning of religion. We are not allowing ourselves the freedom that any critical reflection on truth claims provoked by any classic text demands. Insofar as theological interpretations of religious claims demand, as they do, a critical analysis of all such claims to truth in order to understand even their meaning, theology can aid any interpreter of religion.[49] In one sense, theologians simply render explicit what is implicit in all interpretations of religion: some conscious or unconscious notions of what counts as true, as other or different, as similar or the same, as possible or impossible. If an interpreter believes that religious claims about Ultimate Reality are nonsense, or sick, or meaningless, or purely epiphenomenal, then she should say so—and argue why others should agree. If the interpreter believes that religious claims are meaningful and true, or possible, or even probable, again he should say so—and argue why others should agree. To demand less is to refuse to interpret the religious classics as the kind of texts they are.

Here too, as in the interpretations of all classics, everything is at risk: the interpreter's present understanding and expectations, the text's former receptions and its central claim to meaning and truth, and the very questioning that is the conversation itself. Any interpreter of the religious classics should admit that all we can hope for is some relatively adequate interpretations of these disturbing texts. And our present interpretations in their turn will become relatively inadequate when further questions and further insights emerge. Why should the interpretation of religion, and it alone, be absolved from these hermeneutical demands? Whether that absolution comes from dogmatists within or outside the religions matters very little. There is no absolution for any interpreter of religion from the full struggle to understand by conversing with the religious classics.

In the interpretation of religion, the problem called reductionism is real. Yet that problem is not solved by refusing to try any method of explanation (sociology of religion, psychology of religion, anthropology of religion), or any hermeneutic of critique (Hume, Voltaire, Feuerbach, Dewey), or any hermeneutic of suspicion (Freud, Marx, Nietzsche, Darwin, feminism), or any hermeneutic of retrieval (Barth, Eliade, Jung, Rahner).[50] Any of these may illuminate some unnoticed or repressed aspect of the complex reality revealed by conversation with the religious classic.

The problem of reductionism is perhaps more accurately described as one of totalization: only this method, or only this hermeneutic of retrieval, or only this critique, or only this hermeneutic of suspicion can interpret what religion really is. Believers, to be sure, have their own reductionist temptations: the claim, for example, that only a hermeneutics of confessionalist retrieval can be allowed to count. In that case, reductionism has a heyday. Under this banner, we can apparently retrieve anything—however repressive or nonsensical. Dogmas are always right; mystery is always present; retrievability is always in order. These are the temptations of any hermeneutic of pure retrieval. They are as much temptations—not necessities—as one of the more familiar candidates for reductionism: the effort of some methods of critique and some hermeneutics of suspicion to explain away religion by ignoring its distinctiveness and insisting that it is really something else, preferably something more familiar and manageable. Religion is then explained totally as an epiphenomenon, which temporally stands in for the really real: society and its needs to affirm itself, the psyche and its demands, the economy and its controls. All methods of reductionism, whether by believers or nonbelievers, are grounded in an unacknowledged confession of their own: the belief that so secure is their present knowledge of truth and possibility that the religious classics can at best be peculiar expressions of more of the same. Anything different, other, alien must clearly be untrue and impossible—that "goes without saying."

These conflicting reductionist procedures are temptations that in a hundred forms beset every interpreter of religion. Hiding within all of them are some secret presuppositions. In some methods and hermeneutics of suspicion there lives the belief that we moderns and postmoderns, as the vanguard of social evolution, have finally discovered the one argument, the one method, the one critical theory that explains all—and explains it usually as more of what we already knew. Impelling all purely traditionalist notions of theology is the shadow side of the same secret belief. We true believers, and we alone, have not ceded to the demands of cultural change. We alone have remained pure and innocent, treating modernity with the contempt it deserves. We are the tradition, and the tradition is pure. *Il Duce ha sempre ragione,* as they used to say in Mussolini's Italy.

The difference between fundamentalist readings and secularist readings seem startling. But these are surface differences of answers, not of fundamental hermeneutical approaches. The Cartesian certainty of some Enlightenment critiques of religion was well matched by the use of the same kind of rationalist methods by some Christian neo-Scholastics in the "Christianity Made Reasonable" texts of that period. Most of us still read the conflicting interpretations of Hume and Butler, for example, since both of them transcended the obsession with certainty of their contemporaries. But who still reads the textbook deists? Or d'Holbach with his bizarre certainty? Or the neo-Scholastics of the manuals? They are, one and all, reverse sides of the same effaced coin of certainty, mastery, and control. The certainty of contemporary positivist and empiricist critiques of religion is well matched by the literalism and fundamentalism of religious dogmatists in all traditions. But besides these more strictly intellectual difficulties, there is another problem: patrons of certainty and control in the interpretation of religion are boring. And whatever else religion is, it is not boring. It is other, different, disturbing. It is not more of the same.

Every interpretation, as interpretation, is an exercise in practical application.[51] In traditional hermeneutical terms, without some *applicatio,* there is no real hermeneutical *intelligentia* or *explicatio.* In that sense the contemporary hermeneutical concern with praxis is entirely correct. If, however, that concern becomes an attempt to free interpreters from the demands of theory or the fuller complexities of interpretation, then praxis itself has become one more inadequate theory. Ironically, praxis then becomes merely the latest in a long line of attempts to free interpreters from understanding history and the practical responsibilities that one's historical moment imposes. When any interpretation of any religious classic is relatively adequate, it inevitably becomes practical as well.[52]

The hermeneutical attempts of some contemporary Christian and Jewish theologies to become both mystical and political are interesting examples of attempts at meeting the full demands of theological interpretation.[53] Historically, neo-Confucianism's extraordinary ability, especially in Wang-Yang Ming, to unite the mystical concerns of classical Taoism and Chan Buddhism with the ethical-political civic concerns of classical Confucianism remains, perhaps, the best historical example of a mystical-political model among all the religions.[54] Many Christian and Jewish theologies of our day are, in effect, attempting to create analogous mystical-political theologies. Consider, for example, how several different Christian theologies now insist on the need for practical application of a mystical-political sort in all theology. Rightly suspicious of the elitism of much academic theological discourse, these groups can sometimes resist discussions of interpretation theory while developing active practical hermeneutics for Christian theology.

These options range widely:[55] "street theologies" that narrate the lives of different Christian groups; the resurgence of social-justice concerns in many evangelical theologies; the radical mystical-political turn of many monastic communities; the liberation theologies of the base communities of the Third World; the calls for communal solidarity among the embattled Christian communities of Eastern and Central Europe. All these practical theologies have considerable import for all academic theologians and, by extension, all interpreters of religion.

Among the lessons they teach is the following: It makes little sense to claim that only a scholarly elite can interpret the religious classics. To suggest that only those who know the latest historical critical or literary critical methods or the most recent debates in hermeneutical theory can properly interpret the scriptures, is like saying that only classical scholars can understand Homer, only Elizabethan specialists can interpret Shakespeare, only film critics can explain Bergman, only musicologists can experience Janis Joplin, only philosophers can learn from Gramsci, and only academic theologians can understand Ibn-Rushid,

Moses Maimonides, and Aquinas. So many onlys, so many property rights in academic notions of proper readings. So many rules on what a competence to read means. Even Louis XIV might have been embarrassed.

There is a natural hermeneutical competence. That competence does not wait upon the results of debates over methods and hermeneutical theories. That natural competence belongs to all those who assume that, to understand any classic and its claim to attention, we must be prepared to risk our present understanding. That competence knows that we cannot simply distance ourselves from the classics as objects-out-there available for either passive contemplation or domination by means of the latest method. It is the competence of anyone willing to confront critically and be confronted by any classic.

There can also be a natural religious competence that may illuminate the interpretation of the religious classics far more than even the most helpful modern techniques. In that sense, what the liberation theologians insist upon is hermeneutically sound. It is this: If the religious classics are both classics and religious at all, they should be intelligible to all. Moreover, the liberationists also insist, if the classics in question are the prophetic classics of Judaism and Christianity, they should also reveal that Ultimate Reality itself has manifested a preference: the preference of the God of the prophets for the poor, the oppressed, the marginalized ones.

How those preferred ones read the scriptural texts in their own situation becomes imperative for all interpreters to hear. It was, after all, the black slaves, not their white masters, who rightly interpreted the heart of the liberation narrative of Exodus. God's option for the poor is central to the Scriptures. This is not to say that option for the poor is translatable into the distinct claim that only the poor can provide proper readings of these texts, any more than it suggests that only the poor can experience revelation or find salvation or only the poor are the objects of that radical love of neighbor that is the heart of the Christian gospel. That option does not translate into the position that says, once the poor make their interpretations, all others are to sit back and passively receive them.[56] In that case, are these new and conflictual readings heard at all? Such passive receptions are engendered by conflict, fear, and guilt, not responsibility. They mask a patronizing anxiety that is the forgotten underside of all elite claims to mastery and control.

The option for the poor does translate, however, into the insistence that the readings of the oppressed—however different and even uncivil by some tired standards of what can count as civil discourse—must be heard, and preferably heard first. In terms of the Scriptures' own standards, the oppressed are the ones most likely to hear clearly the full religious and political demands of the prophets. Among our contemporaries, their readings are those the rest of us most need to hear. Through their interpretations and actions, we can finally read these texts with new eyes and thereby free ourselves from all idealist readings. The mystical political texts of the prophets, Exodus, and the apocalypses insist upon both spiritual and material liberation. Recall the prophets' judgments on Israel for its treatment of widows, orphans, and the poor; recall the Gospels' portrayal of Jesus as the friend of the outcasts of his day. Christian salvation is not exhausted by any program of political liberation, to be sure, but Christian salvation, rightly understood, cannot be divorced from the struggle for total human liberation—individual, social, political, and religious.[57]

As these new readings by and for the oppressed are heard by all theologians and, in principle, by all interpreters of religion, a yet-deeper sense of our own plurality and ambiguity will surface and give rise to further conflicts of interpretations over the religious classics. Beyond the questions of the sexism, racism, classism, and anti-Semitism in the Christian classics and their history of effects upon all interpretations, lies a further disturbing question: is there yet another illusion systemically operative in much theological discourse—the belief, rarely expressed, but often acted upon, that only a learned elite can read these texts properly? For these texts are "our" property. All who wish to enter the discussion should leave the margins and come to the centers to receive the proper credentials. They must earn property rights if they are to fashion proper readings of the religious classics.

This kind of unconscious elitism, I have come to believe, is not a mere error. Like other distortions, elitism is both unconscious and systemic. It is a distortion whose power will be broken only when we learn to hear these alternative readings of the oppressed. The most powerful acts of resistance are often those where the first lesson is to resist oneself. Many interpreters of religion have begun to learn that lesson on racism, sexism, classism, and anti-Semitism. It is time to learn the same kind of lesson on elitism. Otherwise we shall hear only ourselves once again as we head down the long slide from liberal guilt to virtual nonresistance to acceptance of the status quo. The ego of the academic theologian, like that of all postmodern intellectuals, needs to learn better ways to dispossess itself of its sense of having exclusive rights to interpretation. Through attending to the readings and actions of the oppressed, postmodern intellectuals may learn to become not alienated egos but human subjects in active solidarity with all those others we have too often presumed to speak for.

I do not here mean that anyone should engage in yet another performance of that drama of official Marxist-Leninist ideology in which intellectuals are obliged to abandon their bourgeois critical role so that the ever-elusive central character, the proletariat, can have its role taken over by the Party. The history of oppression imposed upon Eastern-bloc peoples should be more than sufficient evidence to distrust Communist promises of liberation. Liberation for whom? The Jews, evangelicals, dissident Orthodox and Catholics? The Muslims in Afghanistan? The peoples throughout Eastern and Central Europe?

The last thing any of us need is another exercise in selective compassion by either right or left. That selectivity characterizes the right when, for example, they never tire of explaining how, alas, we cannot now express our resistance to the intolerable injustices inflicted upon individuals and whole peoples by such regimes as those in South Africa, Guatemala, Paraguay, and Chile, or even pay much attention to the injustices imposed by our own system upon the poor and the marginalized in the Western democracies, because we must direct all our energies against the undeniable outrages caused by our ideological opponents.

That same objectionable selectivity can characterize the left as well: whenever, for example, they focus their considerable compassion and sense of justice upon certain oppressed groups at the expense of others—witness the rarely interrupted silence of the left on what is happening to individuals and groups in

Czechoslovakia or Romania or the Soviet Union itself. The left, too, too often seem to live by a puzzling selectivity. But selective compassion will not do. As Camus once observed:

But it seems to me that there is another ambition that ought to belong to all writers: to bear witness and shout aloud: every time it is possible, insofar as our talent allows, for those who are enslaved. . . . That is the very ambition you questioned in your article, and I shall consistently refuse you the right to question it, so long as the murder of a man angers you only when that man shares your ideas.[58]

To hear the readings of the oppressed means that the rest of us need to acknowledge the ambiguity of the relationships of power and knowledge in our own discourse. We should not, for example, simply turn these new interpretations and actions by the oppressed into suggestive possibilities—as modern aesthetes have turned Brecht's alienation effects into one more modernist classic now labeled "Brechtian." The final indignity for anyone is to be forbidden one's own voice or to be robbed of one's own experience. To learn to listen is a good first lesson for all interpreters of the religious classics to keep in mind when hearing these new conflictual interpretations of the oppressed. Of course, that imperative to listen cannot be the final word. If criticism and suspicion stop there, what really has been accomplished? Something, perhaps: a correct religious sense of our guilt and our need for repentance—but not a critical response or an active solidarity. Responsibility demands critical conflict when necessary and resistance, including resistance to these new interpretations, when appropriate.

For example, in my judgment we should resist any claim from any Third World theologian that the classic liberal rights of freedom of speech, religion, press, assembly, and so on are no longer important for the dialectic of history and merit no theological defense. Any dialectic that can reject those genuine accomplishments of the bourgeois revolutions should be resisted. On the whole and considering the alternatives, these values of the Western bourgeois democracies are worth defending theologically, while attempting at the same time to transform them, guided by the Western democratic tradition's own too often betrayed ideals.[59] For us genuinely to listen to the voices of the Third World theologians, as well as the Second-World theologians, is to hear demands for far more transformation than most of us in the so-called First World have yet imagined. But to hear those voices is also to resist them when necessary and to insist upon the lesson that their own emphasis on conflict can teach anew: every conversation, if it is worthy of being named a conversation at all, will not shun necessary moments of conflict; every response to their readings must be critical and active, not passively receptive.

Resistance can take as many forms as the plural interpretations empowering that resistance. For some writers and scholars, it may happen behind their backs—as it happens in any good historical work which shows how what seems so natural to us now actually came to be. For others, resistance can take the self-conscious form of critical thought in the interest of emancipation: as in the critical theorists of Frankfurt; the ethical-political probings of such literary scholars as Kenneth Burke, Wayne Booth, Edward Said, Terry Eagleton, and Frank Lentricchia;[60] the mystical-political thrust of such different theologians as Johann Baptist Metz, Jürgen Moltmann, Rosemary Radford Ruether, James Cone, Emil Fackenheim, or Elisabeth Schüssler Fiorenza.[61] It remains true that not to choose is itself a choice. And not to realize that true understanding includes practical application is itself a form of inadequate understanding.

All seemingly apolitical readings of the religious classics are as influenced by society and history as any self-consciously ethical-political reading. They all demand some critical theoretical analysis if they are not to delude themselves with appeals to some pure experience that their own discourse and action will always already betray. For neither the world nor language is pure. The world is what it is and not another thing.

When it is believable, religious faith manifests a sense of the radical mystery of all reality: the mystery we are to ourselves; the mystery of history, nature, and the cosmos; the mystery, above all, of Ultimate Reality.[62] When it is plausible, religious hope frees us from our temperamental inclinations to either pessimism or optimism. When it is active, religious love frees us from the illusion that to be a human being means to become an ego attempting mastery and control of all others. There is no historyless, discourseless human being. There are only the several attempts to become a human being through interpreting critically the different traditions that formed any particular model of self in the first place. There is no "natural religion" freed from the history and discourse of the historical religions. Buddhist compassion is not the same as Christian love. Both present us with models, sometimes complementary, sometimes conflicting, for becoming an authentic human being.

Of course, it is the case that responses to religious classics by believers and nonbelievers will be genuinely different. The believer will sense in the religious classic the interruptive presence of Ultimate Reality empowering a way of life otherwise thought impossible. If this seems unlikely, then read the life of Simone Weil or Dietrich Bonhoeffer.[63] Believers will converse with the tradition in order to be transformed. The ones who partly succeed are named the witnesses, the just, the enlightened ones, the saints.

Believers know that, for others, interpretative responses to the religious classics must inevitably be different. If anyone believes in a revelation of Ultimate Reality in a particular religious tradition, this affects her or his understanding of all reality. Jews, Christians, and Muslims believe in the God attested to by Abraham and Sarah; if they understand that belief rightly, they will not pretend to any control over their always-precarious speech on the Ultimate Reality who is God. They will, of course, strive for as much clarity as possible to understand the one they name God, as process theologians attempt to do in their helpful clarifications of what Christians mean by their central metaphor "God is love."[64]

In and through even the best speech for Ultimate Reality, greater obscurity eventually emerges to manifest a religious sense of that Reality as ultimate mystery. Silence may be the most appropriate kind of speech for evoking this necessary sense of the radical mystery—as mystics insist when they say, "Those who know do not speak; those who speak do not know." The most refined theological discourse of the classic theologians ranges widely but returns at last to a deepened sense of the same ultimate mystery: the amazing freedom with all traditional doctrinal formulations in Meister Eckhart; the confident portrayals of God in Genesis and Exodus become the passionate outbursts of the prophets and the painful reflections of Job, Ecclesiastes, and Lamentations; the disturbing light cast by the biblical metaphors of the "wrath of God" on all temptations to sentimentalize what love means when the believer says, "God is love"; the proclamation of the hidden and revealed God in Luther and Calvin; the *deus otiosus* vision of God in the Gnostic traditions; the repressed discourse of the witches; the startling female imagery for Ultimate Reality in both the great matriarchal traditions and the great Wisdom traditions of both Greeks and Jews; the power of the sacred dialectically divorcing itself from the profane manifested in all religions; the extraordinary subtleties of rabbinic writing on God become the uncanny paradoxes of kabbalistic thought on God's existence in the very materiality of letters and texts; the subtle debates in Hindu philosophical reflections on monism and polytheism; the many faces of the Divine in the stories of Shiva and Krishna; the puzzling sense that, despite all appearances to the contrary, there is "nothing here that is not Zeus" in Aeschylus and Sophocles; the terror caused by Dionysius in Euripides' *Bacchae;* the refusal to cling even to concepts of "God" in order to become free to experience Ultimate Reality as Emptiness in much Buddhist thought; the moving declaration of that wondrous clarifier Thomas Aquinas, "All that I have written is straw; I shall write no more"; Karl Rahner's insistence on the radical incomprehensibility of both God and ourselves understood through and in our most comprehensible philosophical and theological speech; Eberhard Jüngel's powerful theology of the Christian understanding of God; the "God beyond God" language of Paul Tillich and all theologians who acknowledge how deadening traditional God-language can easily become; the refusal to speak God's name in classical Judaism; the insistence on speaking that name in classical Islam; the hesitant musings on the present-absent God in Buber become the courageous attempts to forge new languages for a new covenant with God in the post-*tremendum* theologies of Cohen, Fackenheim, and Greenberg. There is no classic discourse on Ultimate Reality that can be understood as mastering its own speech. If any human discourse gives true testimony to Ultimate Reality, it must necessarily prove uncontrollable and unmasterable.

These examples do not suggest, however, that only believers should attempt to interpret these languages. As my earlier appeal to the language of silence in Wittgenstein and Heidegger— who may or may not have been believers—suggests, anyone willing to risk an interpretation of the religious classics clearly can interpret them. To claim that only believers can interpret the religions, moreover, is a position that ultimately robs the religious classics of their claims to truth. At the limit, that position consigns the religious classics to the private reservation of a bureaucratic elite. The privatization of religion in the modern period, like the marginalization of art and the technicization of politics, is a battered script with a single plot:[65] no classic manifestations will be granted any cognitive status, no interpretations of those classics will be accorded any public claim or allowed to disclose any possibilities other than those we already knew. For what we now know, whether modestly empirical or militantly postitivist, is all that can be known. Any resistance to this knowledge must be made according to those rules, or it quite simply will not count.

Hermann Göring once said that whenever he heard the word *culture*, he reached for his gun; the more benign modern technocrats are tempted to reach for their pocket calculators when they hear the word *religion*. If modern interpreters of the religious classics, whether believers or nonbelievers, wish to claim no public status for the possibilities they interpret, no one will stop them. But before they fall back into passive contemplations, they should acknowledge the price they are prepared to pay. That price is the one the romantics were eventually forced to pay: a concept of creativity wedded to a belief in purely personal expression. Despite their own noble intentions to resist a then-reigning mechanism, the romantics found themselves forced into private reservations of the spirit. The price of privacy for religion, art, and thought alike is that all the classics will be rounded up and placed in harmless reservations of the spirit by all those who know the game of power—the sanctimonious bureaucrats in all the religions, those who fashion reputations in the art world, and the official intellectual minions of capitalist and socialist societies alike.

As I suspect is clear by now, I do believe in belief. I believe that faith in Ultimate Reality can make all the difference for a life of resistance, hope, and action. I believe in God. It is, I confess, that belief which gives me hope. At the same time, I do not believe in confining the interpretation of the religious classics to believers alone. If the religious classics are classics at all, they can be trusted to evoke a wide range of responses. On a spectrum, the responses can range from the shock of recognition religiously named faith, as radical trust in, and loyalty to, Ultimate Reality, to some far more tentative religious sense that, without implying belief, can nevertheless envisage some enlightenment and emancipation in the religious classics.

Whatever their radical differences in interpretation, neither the theologians of retrieval nor the posttheologians of suspicion have allowed themselves the option of simply changing the subject when they encountered the limit questions evoked by any authentic conversation with the religious classics. That option was left to the complacency of modern empiricist culture. It was left to those whose only form of resistance is to change the subject. But that subject, once changed, further impoverishes an already-embattled human subject. The fundamental questions to which the religious classics respond cannot be so easily set aside. As long as human beings question their most profound joys and their deepest anxieties, they remain open to the need for some enlightenment, some emancipation. The alternative is yet another superfluous vote in the endless plebiscite conducted by the unrelenting enforcers of more of the same.

Whitehead once suggested that a religious sensibility begins with a sense that "something is awry." In ways that Whitehead could not have foreseen, we now sense that something may be very awry indeed in all our classics and traditions, including the religious ones. No great religion should hesitate to apply to itself its own suspicion of either sin or ignorance. As surely as there are religious hermeneutics of retrieval, there are also religious hermeneutics of suspicion to uncover what may be awry in the religion itself. The prophetic strands in any religion are the clearest examples of such religious suspicion, as Kierkegaard's *Attack Upon Christendom* amply demonstrates.[66] But the prophets do not stand alone; the great mystics have also fashioned powerful hermeneutics of religious suspicion.[67] Why otherwise the paradoxical language of the koans in Zen writings? Why the ceaseless attempts to reformulate the stages for the mystical journey in Teresa of Avila? Why her warnings on ecstasies and visions? Why the insistence in John of the Cross that a dark night of the soul awaits any attempt to follow the mystical way? Why all this if a religious hermeneutics of suspicion does not exist within religion itself?

These strategies of both retrieval and suspicion, and often retrieval through suspicion, should also free religious persons and traditions to open themselves to other hermeneutics of critique and suspicion, whatever their source. For believers to be unable to learn from secular feminists on the patriarchal nature of most religions or to be unwilling to be challenged by Feuerbach, Darwin, Marx, Freud, or Nietzsche is to refuse to take seriously the religion's own suspicions on the existence of those fundamental distortions named sin, ignorance, or illusion. The interpretations of believers will, of course, be grounded in some fundamental trust in, and loyalty to, the Ultimate Reality both disclosed and concealed in one's own religious tradition. But fundamental trust, as any experience of friendship can teach, is not immune to either criticism or suspicion. A religious person will ordinarily fashion some hermeneutics of trust, even one of friendship and love, for the religious classics of her or his tradition.[68] But, as any genuine understanding of friendship shows, friendship often demands both critique and suspicion. A belief in a pure and innocent love is one of the less happy inventions of the romantics. A friendship that never includes critique and even, when appropriate, suspicion is a friendship barely removed from the polite and wary communication of strangers. As Buber showed, in every I-thou encounter, however transient, we encounter some new dimension of reality.[69] But if that encounter is to prove more than transitory, the difficult ways of friendship need a trust powerful enough to risk itself in critique and suspicion. To claim that this may be true of all our other loves but not true of our love for, and trust in, our religious tradition makes very little sense either hermeneutically or religiously.

We find ourselves, therefore, with a plurality of interpretations and methods. We find ourselves with diverse religious classics among many religious traditions. We find ourselves glimpsing the plurality within each tradition while also admitting the ambiguity of every religion: liberating possibilities to be retrieved, errors to be criticized, unconscious distortions to be unmasked.

The attempt to understand remains an effort to interpret

well. But to interpret as pluralistic, ambiguous, and important a phenomenon as religion is to enter a conflict of interpretations from which there can often seem no exit. The conflicts on how to interpret religion, the conflicts caused by the opposing claims of the religions themselves, and the internal conflicts within any great religion all affect interpreters, whether they will it or not. None of these conflicts is easily resolved, and no claim to certainty, whether religionist or secularist, should pretend otherwise.

We can continue to give ourselves over to the great hope of Western reason. But that hope is now a more modest one as a result of the discovery of the plurality of both language and knowledge and the ambiguities of all histories, including the history of reason itself.[70] And yet that hope of reason—a hope expressed, for Westerners, in the models of conversation and argument first created by the Greeks—still lives through any honest fidelity to the classic Socratic imperative, "The unreflective life is not worth living."

We can continue to give ourselves over to the hopes alive in all the great religions: a trust in Ultimate Reality, a hope for the ability to resist what must be resisted, a hope in hope itself, a hope that fights against our exhausted notions of what hope might be. For most religious believers,[71] that hope arises from the belief that Ultimate Reality is grace-ful. For nonbelieving interpreters of the religious classics, that hope may be glimpsed in the religious classics by sensing some enlightenment, however tentative, and some Utopian possibility of emancipation, however modest. The hope proclaimed by all religious ways is well expressed by the classic Buddhist apothegm, "The unlived life is not worth reflecting upon."

What conversation is to the life of understanding, solidarity must be to the life of action. Both conversation and solidarity, like reason itself, are grounded in real hopes: a hope for freedom from the rule of the same and a hope for some enlightenment and emancipation. As I suspect is obvious by now, my own hope is grounded in a Christian faith that revelations from God have occurred and that there are ways to authentic liberation. I believe that such a trust is reasonable, but it is not my purpose here to engage in the necessarily lengthy defense required by that option.[72]

For whether I have good reasons for my Christian hope is another story than the one I have attempted to tell here. Rather, my principal concern in this narrative has been to describe a more modest but crucial hope, and one suggested by the conflict of interpretations on interpretation itself. That hope is this: that all those involved in interpreting our situation and all those aware of our need for solidarity may continue to risk interpreting all the classics of all the traditions. And in that effort to interpret lie both resistance and hope.

Einstein once remarked that with the arrival of the atomic age everything had changed except our thinking. Unfortunately the remark is true. Perhaps contemporary reflections on interpretation, with their emphasis on plurality and ambiguity, are one more stumbling start, across the disciplines, to try to change our usual ways of thinking. It is true that the point is not to interpret the world but to change it. But we will change too little, and that probably too late, if we do not at the same time change our understanding of what we mean when we so easily claim to interpret the world. Our Western dreams of domination, mastery, and certainty are over. The hope that interpretation will show us a way to resist is a fragile hope in a nuclear age. It may be less than we deserve, but it may also be more than we usually allow ourselves to envision, much less act upon.

As for the rest, there is no release for any of us from the conflict of interpretations if we would understand at all. The alternative is not an escape into the transient pleasures of irony or a flight into despair and cynicism. The alternative is not a new kind of innocence or a passivity masking apathy. Whoever fights for hope, fights on behalf of us all. Whoever acts on that hope, acts in a manner worthy of a human being. And whoever so acts, I believe, acts in a manner faintly suggestive of the reality and power of that God in whose image human beings were formed to resist, to think, and to act. The rest is prayer, observance, discipline, conversation, and actions of solidarity-in-hope. Or the rest is silence.

Notes

CHAPTER 1: INTERPRETATION, CONVERSATION, ARGUMENT

1. For the details of the controversy, see Robert Darnton, "Danton and Double-Entendre," *New York Review of Books* 31, 2: 19–24.
2. For the debates and bibliographies on the Revolution, see J. McManners, "The Historiography of the French Revolution," in *The New Cambridge Modern History VIII: The American and French Revolutions, 1763–93* (Cambridge: Cambridge University Press, 1965); François Furet, *Penser la Révolution française* (Paris: Gallimard, 1983); William Doyle, *The Origins of the French Revolution* (Oxford: Oxford University Press, 1980), 7–40. For analyses of responses by artists to the Revolution, see Jean Starobinski, *1789: The Emblems of Reason* (Charlottesville, VA: University of Virginia Press, 1984), and Ronald Paulsen, *Representations of Revolution 1789–1820*, (New Haven, CT: Yale University Press, 1983).
3. For these methodological debates in relationship to the revolution, see Michael Keith Baker, "On the Problem of the Ideological Origins of the French Revolution," in *Modern European Intellectual History; Reappraisals and New Perspectives*, ed. Dominick LaCapra and Steven L. Kaplan (Ithaca, NY: Cornell University Press, 1982), 197–220.
4. Readers of Bernard Lonergan's great work *Insight: A Study of Human Understanding* (London: Longmans, Green, 1957) will recognize his presence here and elsewhere in this work—a presence for which I remain all the more thankful despite the obvious differences on "language" and understanding and thereby interpretation.
5. See Kenneth Burke, *The Philosophy of Literary Form: Studies in Symbolic Action* (Berkeley and Los Angeles: University of California Press, 1957), 259–61; and, for examples of his fidelity to this principle, *A Grammar of Motives* (New York: Prentice-Hall, 1945); *Rhetoric of Motives* (Berkeley and Los Angeles: University of California Press, 1969).
6. In this and in the following sections, the work of Hans-Georg Gadamer on interpretation is prominent; inter alia, see especially *Truth and Method* (New York: Seabury, 1975); *Dialogue and Dialectic: Eight Hermeneutical Studies in Plato* (New Haven, CT: Yale University Press, 1980); *Philosophical Hermeneutics* (Berkeley and Los Angeles: University of California Press, 1976); *The Idea of the Good in The Platonic-Aristotelian Philosophy*, ed. P. Christopher Smith (New Haven, CT: Yale University Press, 1986). A good study of Gadamer may be found in Joel C. Weisheimer, *Gadamer's Hermeneutics: A Reading of Truth and Method* (New Haven, CT: Yale University Press, 1985). Readers of Gadamer will note that, besides the more obvious differences on argument, explanation, critique, and suspicion (as distinct from retrieval) between my position and his, the analysis I give of interpretation-as-conversation, although clearly indebted to Gadamer's pioneering work, is less directed than his to an ontology of understanding and

more to developing an empirical (Anglo-American?) model for the interpretation of texts; these two enterprises are not, I believe, divisive, but they are clearly distinct. The basic analysis of conversation in Gadamer may be found in *Truth and Method*, 325–45.

7. It should be noted that the recent revival of Aristotle is largely concerned not with his notions of demonstrative science (in the *Prior Analytic*) but with his notions of argument in dialectic and rhetoric. In dialectic, syllogism and generalizations play the major role; in rhetoric, enthymenes and examples. On the difficulties in Aristotle's notion of science, see Bernard Lonergan, "Aquinas Today: Tradition and Innovation," in *A Third Collection: Papers by Bernard J. Lonergan, S. J.*, ed. Frederick E. Crowe, S. J. (New York: Paulist, 1985), 35–55.

8. I have defended this notion of the "classic" in *The Analogical Imagination: Christian Theology and the Culture of Pluralism* (New York: Crossroads, 1981), 99–154. It may be worth repeating that my own major hermeneutical interest lies in the reception of the classic—a problem distinct from both the production of the classic and empirical-historical analyses of the role of classics in the shifting canons of the culture. Hans-Robert Jauss's work in reception theory is illuminating on the question; although I continue to prefer my own formulation of the question, Jauss's suggestions (especially on the spectrum of responses) elaborate the same fundamental view; see especially his *Toward an Aesthetic of Reception* (Minneapolis: University of Minnesota Press, 1982).

Critics who continue to read any defense of the category "classic" as, in effect, a defense of classicism or even of pure retrieval, disallowing explanatory theories and suspicion (as in most of Gadamer's own uses of the notion), have not reflected much on what the notion, as here employed, actually means or even, it would seem, on the role of examples in Aristotle become, as here, the role of those "exemplary examples," the classics. For an analogous defense of the category "classic" also accompanied by a challenge to classicist readings, see Frank Kermode, *The Classic* (New York: Harcourt, Brace, Jovanovich, 1975).

9. On the question of canons, see "Canons," the special issue of *Critical Inquiry* 10 (Sept. 1983).

10. As one example among many kinds of studies now available on this question, see Richard Jenkyns, *The Victorians and Ancient Greece* (Cambridge, MA: Harvard University Press, 1980).

11. See Northrop Frye, *The Great Code* (New York: Harcourt, Brace, Jovanovich, 1981), and Herbert Schneidau, *Sacred Discontent: The Bible and Western Tradition* (Berkeley and Los Angeles: University of California Press, 1976). For the role of the Bible in the Christian church, see Robert Grant with David Tracy, *A Short History of the Interpretation of the Bible* (Philadelphia: Fortress, 1984).

12. Inter alia, see E. P. Sanders, *Paul and Palestinian Judaism: A Comparison of Patterns of Religion* (Philadelphia: Fortress, 1977).

13. For the last category, see Hans Frei, *The Eclipse of Biblical Narrative* (New Haven, CT: Yale University Press, 1974), and his constructive theology in *The Identity of Jesus Christ* (Philadelphia: Fortress, 1975).

14. Such reception may be studied from the viewpoint of different disciplines: either in literary and historical terms, as in the works cited in nn. 10 and 11; or in sociological terms, as in Arnold Hauser, *The Social History of Art* (London: Routledge and Kegan Paul, 1968); or in hermeneutical-philosophical terms, as in Hans-Robert Jauss, *Toward an Aesthetic of Reception*. As examples of works that unite several of these perspectives, see George Steiner, *Antigones* (Oxford: Oxford University Press, 1984), and Michael Walzer, *Exodus and Revolution* (New York: Basic Books, 1985).

15. Contemporary philosophers who have addressed this issue of the "other" (prominent since the dialectic in Hegel's *Phenomenology of Spirit*) are studied in

Michael Theunissen, *The Other: Studies in the Social Ontology of Husserl, Heidegger, Sartre and Buber* (Cambridge, MA: MIT Press, 1984). Special attention should be given to the extraordinary study of Emmanuel Levinas, *Totality and Infinity* (Pittsburgh: Duquesne University Press, 1969). For an alternative view, see Jacques Derrida, *The Ear of the Other,* ed. Christie V. McDonald (New York: Schocken Books, 1982), and "Violence and Metaphysics: An Essay on the Thought of Emmanuel Levinas," in *Writing and Difference* (Chicago: University of Chicago Press, 1978), 70–154; and Jacques Lacan, especially *Écrits: A Selection* (New York: Norton, 1977).

16. To read a great interpreter of the classics is to recognize this kind of difference immediately; see, for example, David Grene's outstanding study of Thucydides and Plato in *Greek Political Theory: The Image of Man in Thucydides and Plato* (Chicago: University of Chicago Press, 1967).

17. On the meaning and truth of this controversial principle, see Hans-Georg Gadamer, *Truth and Method,* 235–345.

18. This is not equivalent to claiming that nothing in the Enlightenment notion of "autonomy" is retrievable; it is, however, equivalent to saying, as the later work of Jürgen Habermas makes clear, that any philosopher who wishes to defend that model must abandon (as Habermas has) any model of a purely autonomous ego established by *any* philosophy of consciousness and attempt (again, as Habermas through his various formulations has) sociologically informed discourse analysis of the limited but real possibilities of "autonomy" and rationality. For Habermas's most recent formulation in this line, see his *Theorie des kommunikativen Handelns,* 2 vols. (Frankfurt, 1981), trans. Thomas McCarthy as *The Theory of Communicative Action* (vol. 1, Boston: Beacon Press, 1984; vol. 2, forthcoming); as well as his acknowledgment that no philosophy of consciousness can meet the problems posed by the early Frankfurt school's "dialectic of enlightenment." For the latter, see Max Horkheimer and Theodor Adorno, *Dialectic of Enlightenment* (New York: Herder and Herder, 1972).

19. On the category "preunderstanding," see Hans-Georg Gadamer, *Truth and Method,* 235–74. On the category "expectation," see Hans-Robert Jauss, "Literary History as a Challenge to Literary Theory," in *Toward an Aesthetic of Reception,* 3–46.

20. See Gadamer, *Truth and Method,* 91–119. Wittgenstein, for whom the category "game" is also central, is far more reluctant, for his usual reasons, to attempt anything like a definition of "game"; see *Philosophical Investigations* (London: Basil, Blackwell, and Mott, 1958), esp. 4–20. The classical historical study remains Johan Huizinga, *Homo Ludens* (Boston: Beacon Press, 1955).

21. Recall, as well, the role of athletics in Greek *paideia*—a role defended by both Plato and Aristotle. See Werner Jaeger, *Paideia: The Ideals of Greek Culture* (New York: Oxford University Press, 1945), 1:205–210.

22. See Ervin Goffman, inter alia, *Relations in Public: Microstudies of the Public Order* (New York: Harper & Row, 1972).

23. Recall the central use of Rilke's poem in Gadamer's preface to *Truth and Method.*

24. See Hans-Georg Gadamer, *Dialogue and Dialectic,* esp. 39–73; see also the interesting interpretation of Plato's development of dialogue in Eric Voegelin, *Plato and Aristotle* (New Orleans: Louisiana University Press, 1957), 3–24; Paul Friedländer, *Plato, An Introduction* (Princeton, NJ: Princeton University Press, 1969), 154–71; and Herman Sinaiko, *Love, Knowledge and Discourse in Plato* (Chicago: University of Chicago Press, 1965). See also the forthcoming work of Professor Kenneth Seeskin, *Dialogue and Discovery: A Study in Socratic Method* (Albany, NY: SUNY Press, 1987).

25. See Tom Stoppard, *Travesties* (New York: Grove, 1975).

26. For example, the dominance of psychology in our culture can destroy the pos-

sibility of allowing the question at stake to take over by an obsession with the psychology of the conversation partners ("I hear what you say" too often becomes "I infer that you don't mean the idea that you say but mean to express a repressed feeling"; this may, of course, be true but is another conversation than the one originally engaged in). Thrasymachus in *Republic* seems a very passionate and angry man who could use some psychological analysis; he also is stating a position on justice that merits consideration as such.

27. Aristotle, *Nichomachean Ethics*, trans. and ed. David Ross (Oxford: Oxford University Press, 1984), bks. 8 and 9.

28. I understand my summary in the text to be in basic harmony with the position on the implicit validity claims in all communication defended by Karl-Otto Apel and Jürgen Habermas. Their position could be clearer, I believe, if they attended more to the wider (necessarily looser) category "conversation" and then related that to their seemingly preferred (but not sole) candidate for communication, namely, "argument." Plato, I believe, knew this, as his increasing appeal in the later dialogues to story and even myth without forfeiting the need for argument shows. Perhaps even the great master of argument, Aristotle, might agree; if his lost dialogues ever emerge again, we shall one day know. The failure in Habermas to provide other than an "autonomous expressive" place for art, little place for myth or symbol, and very little place for religion suggests that his communication theory, however persuasive on scientific and ethical rationality, seems to have serious problems with art, myth, and religion. Perhaps it would be useful, therefore, for a reopening of the famous Gadamer-Habermas debate—this time on the question of the truth claim of art, myth, and religion and thereby of the model of conversation as more helpful for understanding human communication than the model of explicit argument. For the earlier debate, see Paul Ricoeur, "Ethics and Culture: Habermas and Gadamer in Dialogue," *Philosophy Today* (1973): 153–65.

29. See Bernard Lonergan, *Method In Theology* (New York: Seabury, 1972), 231.

30. I have tried to clarify and defend this category in *The Analogical Imagination*, esp. 446–57, and in "The Analogical Imagination in Catholic Theology," in John Cobb and David Tracy, *Talking About God: Doing Theology in the Context of Modern Pluralism* (New York: Paulist, 1983), 17–29.

31. Cobb and Tracy, *Talking About God*, 29–39.

32. Rudolf Otto, *The Idea of the Holy* (Oxford: Oxford University Press, 1971).

33. Samuel T. Coleridge, *Biographia Literaria* (London: J. M. Dent & Sons, 1965), 167.

34. Indicative of this postmodernist sensibility is the rehabilitation of allegory, especially in Walter Benjamin, *The Origin of German Tragic Drama* (London: Schocken, 1977), and Paul de Man, *Allegories of Reading: Figural Language in Rousseau, Nietzsche, Rilke and Proust* (New Haven, CT: Yale University Press, 1979). For the history of allegory, see Michael Murrin, *The Allegorical Epic: Essays in Its Rise and Decline* (Chicago: University of Chicago Press, 1980).

35. Martin Heidegger, "The Origin of the Work of Art" and "Building Dwelling Thinking," in *Basic Writings*, ed. D. Krell (New York: Harper & Row, 1977), 143–89; 319–41. For secondary work, see David Halliburton, *Poetic Thinking: An Approach to Heidegger* (Chicago: University of Chicago Press, 1981); Manfred Frings, ed., *Heidegger and the Quest for Truth* (Chicago: Quadrangle Books, 1968); David A. White, *Heidegger and the Language of Poetry* (Lincoln: University of Nebraska Press, 1978). This is not to say that the Greeks held there was no truth in the work of art; recall Aristotle's discussion of "poetry" and the universal via the particular (in contrast to history) in the *Poetics*. Even Plato, despite his attack on the "poets" and his famous interpretation of art as imitation of imitation, seems anxious to establish new poetry (hymns to the gods and new myths) to bespeak truth. On this much disputed question see Hans-Georg Gadamer,

"Plato and the Poets," in *Dialogue and Dialectic*, 39–73; Iris Murdoch, *The Fire and the Sun: Why Plato Banished the Artists* (Oxford: Oxford University Press, 1977). For a fuller description of the model "disclosure-concealment," see chap. 2.

36. See Hans-Robert Jauss, *Toward an Aesthetic of Reception*, 3–46, 139–89.

37. Emmanuel Levinas, "The Trace of the Other," in *Deconstruction in Context: Literature and Philosophy*, ed. M. C. Taylor (Chicago: University of Chicago Press, 1986).

38. Consider, for example, a response to the work of Céline that anyone is now likely to possess. The importance of ethical considerations here is subtly and not moralistically discussed by Wayne Booth in his forthcoming work on ethical reading.

39. The locus classicus for phronesis remains Aristotle's *Nichomachean Ethics*. In the recent recovery of the importance of phronesis, the work of Richard Bernstein is especially valuable; see *Beyond Objectivism and Relativism: Science, Hermeneutics and Praxis* (Philadelphia: University of Pennsylvania Press, 1983) and *Philosophical Profiles: Essays in a Pragmatic Mode* (Philadelphia: University of Pennsylvania Press, 1986). I wish to express my thanks to Charles Allen, whose work here (on his thesis-in-progress on *phronesis*) is very helpful.

40. See John Dewey, *The Quest for Certainty* (New York: Putnam, 1929).

41. Hilary Putnam, "The Craving for Objectivity," *New Literary History* 15 (Winter 1984): 229–39. See also "Reason and History," in *Reason, Truth and History* (Cambridge: Cambridge University Press, 1981), 150–73.

42. The model of disclosure-concealment (generically manifestation), it should be noted, is not a move to a romantic or an expressive model but recognizes the need for conversation with the work of art itself.

43. The word *occasionally* here is not synonymous with *merely occasionally*; all conversation—including that implicit in every manifestation—implicitly bears validity claims that can be rendered explicit when the occasion warrants it (e.g., a challenge to any claim to recognize a manifestory truth in the work of art).

44. This is, of course, the famous charge of Nietzsche—who remains, I believe, more ambivalent to Socrates than Walter Kaufmann suggests in *Nietzsche: Philosopher, Psychologist, Antichrist* (Princeton, NJ: Princeton University Press, 1974), 391–412, but also more ambivalent to the Sophists than some deconstructionist thinkers believe. Recall, for example, Nietzsche on Socrates and Euripides (and the Sophists) in *The Birth of Tragedy* (New York: Random House, 1967), 76–98. Perhaps this also suggests that, in the texts of Nietzsche, the "new Nietzsche" and the "old Nietzsche" reside more uneasily side by side than many Nietzsche interpreters admit. For the "new Nietzsche," see Gilles Deleuze, *Nietzsche and Philosophy* (New York: Columbia University Press, 1983); Alexander Nehamas, *Nietzsche: Life as Literature* (Cambridge, MA: Harvard University Press 1985) and "Nietzsche's Return," *Semiotexte III*, 1 (1978); and David B. Allison, ed., *The New Nietzsche* (Cambridge, MA: MIT Press, 1985). For the "old Nietzsche," see Kaufmann and Karl Jaspers, *Nietzsche* (Chicago: Henry Regnery, 1966).

45. David Hume, *Dialogues Concerning Natural Religion* (New York: Hafner, 1969). The wonderful irony of Hume is surely one clue here—but only one; see the representative discussions in V. C. Chappell, ed., *Hume: A Collection of Critical Essays* (Garden City, NY: Doubleday, 1966), 361–424. See also John Vladimir Price, *The Ironic Hume* (Austin: University of Texas Press, 1965).

46. For the debates here, see John H. Hick and Arthur C. McGill, eds., *The Many-Faced Argument: Anselm's Ontological Argument* (New York: Macmillan, 1967).

47. See Karl-Otto Apel, *Towards a Transformation of Philosophy* (London: Routledge and Kegan, 1980) and *Understanding and Explanation: A Transcendental-Pragmatic Perspective* (Cambridge, MA: MIT Press, 1984).

48. For two examples of that intuitive power, see Max Scheler, *The Nature of Sympathy* (Hamden, CT: Archon, 1970) and *Ressentiment* (New York: Free Press, 1961).
49. See Stephen Toulmin, *The Uses of Argument* (Cambridge: Cambridge University Press, 1958).
50. Ibid., for the important distinctions between data, claim, warrants and backings, and conclusions in arguments.
51. See Jürgen Habermas, *Communication and the Evolution of Society* (London: Heinemann, 1979).
52. At this point, the call for "local" or specific studies of the relationships of the discourses of truth and the concrete realities of power of Michel Foucault is enlightening; see *Power/Knowledge*, ed. C. Gordon (New York: Pantheon, 1972), and *Power, Truth, Strategy*, ed. Meaghan Morris and Paul Patton (Sydney: Feral Publications, 1979).
53. See Stephen Toulmin, *Human Understanding*, vol 1, *The Collective Use and Evolution of Concepts* (Princeton, NJ: Princeton University Press, 1972), which seems to me subtler in its analysis than the more famous analysis of Thomas Kuhn, *The Structure of Scientific Revolutions* (Chicago: University of Chicago Press, 1962; 2d ed., 1970). For Foucault, see especially *The Order of Things: An Archaeology of the Human Sciences* (London: Random, 1970), as well as his later works on truth and power noted in note 52.
54. See Jürgen Habermas, *Toward a Rational Society* (London: Heinemann, 1970).
55. On Habermas's development, see the study by Thomas McCarthy, *The Critical Theory of Jürgen Habermas* (Cambridge, MA: MIT Press, 1978); Rick Roderick, *Habermas and the Foundations of Critical Theory* (New York: St. Martin's Press, 1986). For a viewpoint against any "transcendental" moves, see Raymond Geuss, *The Idea of a Critical Theory: Habermas and the Frankfurt School* (Cambridge: Cambridge University Press, 1981), esp. 55–96. For a helpful comparative study, see John B. Thompson, *Critical Hermeneutics: A Study in the Thought of Paul Ricoeur and Jürgen Habermas* (Cambridge: Cambridge University Press, 1981).
56. See Charles Hartshorne's constructive and historical arguments in the anthology entitled *Philosophers Speak of God*, ed. Charles Hartshorne and William Reese (Chicago: University of Chicago Press, 1953), and *A Natural Theology for Our Time* (LaSalle, IL: Open Court, 1967). For studies of Hartshorne here, see Donald Wayne Viney, *Charles Hartshorne and the Existence of God* (Albany, NY: State University of New York Press, 1985); George L. Goodwin, *The Ontological Argument of Charles Hartshorne* (Missoula, MT: Scholars Press, 1978).
57. For this reason, I believe that Gadamer's choice of the game of conversation as the model to analyze remains more helpful as a starting point than the more familiar choice of argument—including my own former use of these key terms.

CHAPTER 2: ARGUMENT: METHOD, EXPLANATION, THEORY

1. Here the central work remains Heidegger's and the developments and clarifications of his thought in such thinkers as Gadamer and Ricoeur: inter alia, see the works on Heidegger listed in chap. 1, n. 35. For Heidegger's notion of truth as a happening or event as *Wahrheitsgeschehen* see, inter alia, his lecture entitled *The Essence of Truth* and the essay *Plato's Doctrine of Truth*. See also David Farrell Krell, "Art and Truth in Raging Discord: Heidegger and Nietzsche on the Will to Power," in *Martin Heidegger and the Question of Literature: Toward a Postmodern Literary Hermeneutics*, ed. William V. Spanos (Bloomington, IN: Indiana University Press, 1979), 39–53; and several of the essays in Michael Murray, ed.,

Heidegger and Modern Philosophy (New Haven, CT: Yale University Press, 1978), Otto Poggeler, *Der Denkweg Martin Heideggers* (Tübingen: Neske, 1968), and Albert Hofstadter, *Truth and Art* (New York: Columbia University Press, 1965). It is interesting that Gadamer resists defining truth despite his title *Truth and Method*. The reason seems obvious: truth, for Gadamer, as for Heidegger and, in a different way, for Ricoeur, is fundamentally an event that happens to a subject and is not under the control of any subject. The major difference between Heidegger and Gadamer here is, I believe, the radicality of Heidegger's insistence that every disclosure involves concealment, in contrast to Gadamer's emphasis on truth as event of disclosure. In Ricoeur, see *History and Truth* (Evanston, IL: Northwestern University Press, 1965), 21–81.

2. It is difficult to formulate the language of "manifestation" without seeming to relate this to visual images for knowing based on perceptual rather than linguistic models. As the text insists, however, even this experience-understanding of manifestation must be understood as dialogical and thereby linguistic—although the language needed for such primal experiences and understanding is likely to be the kind Heidegger named meditative rather than calculative. The rediscovery of the language of the mystics and, among several postmodern thinkers, of the language of silence ("Silence is possible only for the speaker"), as well as the linguistic subtleties in Plato's own use of visual metaphors, suggests that a reemphasis on the language of manifestation (more exactly, disclosure/concealment-recognition), if modeled dialogically, need abandon neither the linguistic turn nor the implicit need for the move to further discursive reasoning—especially the further arguments on the implicit validity claims in all manifestations. These later moves remain important: they can discriminate and help to evaluate the earlier moments of manifestation; they cannot replace them.

3. This seems true even for our Greek forebears; witness Heidegger's appeal to the pre-Socratics or even Nietzsche's to Aeschylus or Voegelin's to Plato himself, or even Derrida's and especially Deleuze's to the Sophists. This primordial understanding of truth-as-manifestation seems historically true of the origin of all of the religions (even for the central prophetic trajectories of Judaism, Christianity, and Islam), as Eliade's magisterial work on cosmic manifestation testifies. See Mircea Eliade, inter alia, *The Sacred and the Profane: The Nature of Religion* (New York: Harper & Brothers, 1957): *The Myth of the Eternal Return* (Princeton, NJ: Princeton University Press, 1957); and *A History of Religious Ideas* (Chicago: University of Chicago Press, 1982), *esp. 1:357–74;* and the formulations of a dialectic of manifestation and proclamation in religion by Paul Ricoeur, "Manifestation and Proclamation," *The Journal of the Blaisdell Institute* 12 (Winter 1978) or my own reformulation in *The Analogical Imagination* (New York: Crossroads, 1981), 193–229.

4. This can also be formulated as a "validity claim"—open both to analysis of the presuppositions of all validity claims (Habermas) and to the analysis of reaching a "virtually unconditioned" judgment when there are no further *relevant* questions (Lonergan); both moves would be needed, in principle, for this further move—a move, to repeat, that should not displace the original manifestation but can help to evaluate it further on reasoned, public, communal grounds. For Lonergan's clarification of judgment as a "virtually unconditioned," see *Insight: A Study of Human Understanding* (London: Longmans, Green, 1958), 271–316.

5. It is perhaps confusing to consider "correspondence" in this way, since historically this was not its meaning; the truth retrievable in these ahistorical and prelinguistic formulations of correspondence theories, however, may be found in widespread notions (largely influenced by pragmatism) of truth as consensus of warranted beliefs; see, inter alia, Hilary Putnam, *Reason, Truth and History* (Cambridge: Cambridge University Press, 1981), and Richard Rorty, *Conse-*

quences of Pragmatism (Minneapolis: University of Minnesota Press, 1982). That there is no ahistorical, nonlinguistic correspondence of "subject" and "object" is what modern philosophical studies of the discourse of truth (both Anglo-American analytical and Continental hermeneutical) have clarified; that correspondence can be revised to mean the consensus of warranted beliefs seems clear even in Thomas Kuhn, if not in Feyerabend nor in some of Rorty. On Feyerabend, see *Against Method* (London: NLB, 1975). On Rorty, contrast the essay "Philosophy as a Kind of Writing: An Essay on Derrida" (pp. 90–110) with "Pragmatism, Relativism, and Irrationalism" (pp. 160–76), in *Consequences of Pragmatism*, op.cit.

6. Paul Ricoeur, *Time and Narrative*, vol. 1 (Chicago: University of Chicago Press, 1984).

7. This can be seen, for example, in Plotinus's clarification of some major aspects of Plato's position or in Porphyry on Plotinus himself. The great commentator traditions, like Thomism, do clarify and develop certain major aspects of Thomas Aquinas (for example, on the logical relationships in Thomas's thought), even if they lose some of the more primordial metaphysical or ontological power of Thomas's discourse. For two examples, on *esse*, see inter alia, Etienne Gilson, *History of Christian Philosophy in the Middle Ages* (New York: Random House, 1955), 361–87; on analogy in the commentators and Thomas himself, see, inter alia, George Klubertanz, *St. Thomas Aquinas on Analogy* (Chicago: Loyola University Press, 1960), and Bernard Montagnes, *La Doctrine de l'analogie de l'être d'après St. Thomas d'Aquin* (Louvain: Nauevelcuts, 1963).

8. The major modern work here is Stephen Toulmin, *The Uses of Argument* (Cambridge: Cambridge University Press, 1958). The classic work remains Aristotle's—with the clarification of dialectics in *Topics* and of rhetoric in the *Rhetoric*. The distinction remains a valuable one, which modern rhetoricians would do well to keep in mind to clarify their claims for rhetoric and thereby avoid overclaims. Besides Toulmin's work, see also Chaim Perelman and L. Olbrechts-Tyteca, *The New Rhetoric: A Treatise on Argumentation* (Notre Dame, IN: University of Notre Dame Press, 1969); Wayne Booth, *Modern Dogma and the Rhetoric of Assent* (Chicago: The University of Chicago Press, 1974) and *Critical Understanding* (Chicago: The University of Chicago Press, 1979).

9. Critics of "metaphysics" often miss the care with which modern metaphysical claims are claims to relative, not absolute, adequacy: careful claims like those in Aristotle and careful claims like those in one of the foremost metaphysical thinkers of our period, Charles Hartshorne; see, inter alia, *Creative Synthesis and Philosophic Method* (Lanham, MA: University Press of America, 1970).

10. On this issue of metaphor, read the contrasting studies of Paul Ricoeur, *The Rule of Metaphor* (Toronto: Toronto University Press, 1977), and Jacques Derrida, "White Mythology," in *Margins of Philosophy* (Chicago: University of Chicago Press, 1975).

11. For elegant defenses of the Enlightenment, see Hans Blumenberg, *The Legitimacy of the Modern Age* (Cambridge, MA: MIT Press, 1983); Peter Gay, *The Enlightenment: An Interpretation* (New York: Vintage, 1968). Philosophically and sociologically, Jürgen Habermas's work continues to provide an important defense of the Enlightenment—both against the earlier formulations of the dialectic of Enlightenment in Adorno and Horkheimer and against the purely historical (project of will) position of Rorty and, implicitly, of Blumenberg. See the exchange between Habermas and Rorty in ed. Richard Bernstein, *Habermas and Modernism*, (Cambridge, MA; MIT Press, 1985), 161–77, 192–217. In Christian theology, the work of Trutz Rendtorff is the clearest and most developed here; for example, see "The Modern Age as a Chapter in the History of Christianity: or The Legacy of Historical Consciousness in Present Theology," *Journal of Re-*

ligion 65 (1985): 478–99. My own position, as I trust is clear from the text, both affirms the accomplishments and retrievability of the Enlightenment and attempts to take seriously the "dialectic of enlightenment" (see chap. 4).

12. On "technical reason," see Max Horkheimer, *Eclipse of Reason* (New York: Oxford University Press, 1947).

13. See Jeffrey Hart, *Reactionary Modernism: Technology, Culture and Politics in Weimar and the Third Reich* (Cambridge: Cambridge University Press, 1984).

14. The work of Max Weber here has proved central for much modern analysis—even once (?) revisionary Marxist analysis like Habermas's.

15. See the analysis of Philip Rieff, *The Triumph of the Therapeutic* (New York: Harper & Row, 1966).

16. On hermeneutics and social science, see Paul Ricoeur, *Hermeneutics and the Human Sciences*, ed. and trans. J. B. Thompson (Cambridge: Cambridge University Press, 1981); see also Charles Taylor, *Philosophical Papers 2* (Cambridge: Cambridge University Press, 1985); Fred R. Dallmayr and Thomas A. McCarthy, eds., *Understanding and Social Inquiry* (Notre Dame, IN: University of Notre Dame Press, 1977).

17. See Mary Gerhart and Allan Russell, *Metaphoric Process: The Creation of Scientific and Religious Understanding* (Fort Worth, TX: Texas Christian University Press, 1984).

18. See Clifford Geertz, "Blurred Genres: The Refiguration of Social Thought," in *Local Knowledge: Further Essays in Interpretive Anthropology* (New York: Basic Books, 1983), 19–36.

19. This emerges most clearly in Gadamer's exchanges with Habermas, op.cit. and in Gadamer's usual descriptions of natural science as purely methodical. However, note Gadamer's qualifications on this question in *Reason in the Age of Science* (Cambridge, MA: MIT Press, 1981).

20. Paul Ricoeur, "The Hermeneutical Function of Distanciation," in *Hermeneutics and the Human Sciences*, 131–45.

21. For example, sociological theory should provide distance from our sense of participation in traditions—as in Weber's and Durkheim's classical sociological explanations of the world religions.

22. That other methods, explanations, and theories need analysis for any adequate contemporary interpretation is also clear. My choice of historical-critical and literary-critical methods is intended as exemplary of the problem, certainly not as exhaustive of it. Rather, I am personally persuaded that both sociological methods and theories and ones from the natural sciences (especially biology) are also needed. Even as I remain unpersuaded by the overclaims of "sociobiology," I am persuaded by the kinds of insights and explanations in such differing social theorists as Edward Shils and Anthony Giddens.

23. Hans Frei, *The Eclipse of Biblical Narrative* (New Haven, CT: Yale University Prss, 1974).

24. For one response to this issue, see my *The Analogical Imagination*, 305–39. For one analysis of recent studies, see William Thompson, *The Jesus Debate: A Survey and Synthesis* (New York: Paulist 1985).

25. See Hayden White, *Metahistory: The Historical Imagination in Nineteenth-Century Europe* (Baltimore: Johns Hopkins University Press, 1973) and *Tropics of Discourse: Essays in Cultural Criticism* (Baltimore: Johns Hopkins University Press, 1978).

26. On the "ethics of historical reason," see Van A. Harvey, *The Historian and the Believer* (New York: Macmillan, 1966).

27. See Walter Benjamin, "Theses on the Philosophy of History," in *Illuminations* (New York: Schocken, 1969); Johann Baptist Metz, *Faith in History and Society* (New York: Crossroads, 1980).

28. Hugh Trevor-Roper, *The Last Days of Hitler* (London: Pan Books, 1962).

29. See Norman Perrin, *Rediscovering the Teachings of Jesus* (London: SCM, 1967).

30. Note, however, how intellectual historians of the revolution can, once informed by economic analyses, return with new force to analyze the history of discourse. See Michael Keith Baker, "On the Problem of the Ideological Origins of the French Revolution," in *Modern European Intellectual History Reappraisals and New Perspectives,* ed. Dominick LaCapra and Steven L. Kaplan (Ithaca, NY: Cornell University Press, 1982), 197–220.

31. For examples, see Paul Ricoeur, *Time and Narrative,* vol. I.

32. See Arnaldo Momigliano, "History in an Age of Ideologies," *The American Scholar* (Autumn 1982), 51:495–507.

33. For a basic bibliography on the debates here, see Terry Eagleton, *Literary Theory: An Introduction* (Minneapolis: University of Minnesota Press, 1983): Jonathan Culler, *The Pursuit of Signs: Semiotics, Literature, Deconstruction* (Ithaca, NY: Cornell University Press, 1981); William Ray, *Literary Meaning: From Phenomenology to Deconstruction* (Oxford: Oxford University Press, 1984).

34. This is also true, I believe, of the sophisticated case of Husserl on intentionality in E. D. Hirsch's reformulation of the meaning of an "author's intention"; see *Validity in Interpretation* (New Haven, CT: Yale University Press, 1967). The debate between Gadamer and Hirsch here could be reformulated as a debate between Husserl on intentionality and Heidegger on historicity.

35. For Jauss, see no. 8 in chap. 1; see also the distinct position of Wolfgang Iser, *The Implied Reader* (Baltimore: Johns Hopkins Press, 1974). For reader-response critics, see Jane P. Tompkins, ed., *Reader-Response Criticism: From Formalism to Post-Structuralism* (Baltimore: Johns Hopkins Press, 1980).

36. The recent work of Wayne Booth is exemplary here; note also how a revisionary Marxist interpreter of the ideologies in literary texts, methods and theories like Terry Eagleton can appeal to the need to return to the ethical-political concerns of ancient rhetoric in *Literary Theory: An Introduction,* 194–217.

37. See the recent debates in Paul de Man, *The Resistance to Theory* (Minneapolis: University of Minnesota Press, 1986); W. J. T. Mitchell ed., *Against Theory: Literary Studies and the New Pragmatism* (Chicago: University of Chicago Press, 1985).

38. On Joyce and Mark, see Frank Kermode, *The Genesis of Secrecy* (Cambridge, MA: Harvard University Press, 1979), 55–63. On Rousseau, see Jacques Derrida, *On Grammatology* (Baltimore: Johns Hopkins Press, 1974), 141–229. On Nietzsche, see Jacques Derrida, *Spurs: Nietzsche's Styles* (Chicago: University of Chicago Press, 1978).

39. For Paul Ricoeur's earlier formulation on sense and reference, see *Interpretation Theory: Discourse and the Surplus of Meaning* (Fort Worth, TX: Texas Christian University Press, 1976). For his more refined and developed notion of "refiguration," see his *Time and Narrative,* 3 vol. On text criticism, see Werner Jeanrond, *Text und Interpretation als Kategorien theologischen Denkens* (Tübingen: J. C. B. Mohr, 1986). It should be noted that Ricoeur's later reformulations on "refiguration" (as preferable to "referent") are important qualifications of what the more generic (and possibly confusing) category "referent" does and does not mean here. For present, more generic purposes, with the caution cited above, the category "referent" (which is not, for texts, immediately translatable into concerns with words and sentences) can suffice.

40. I have taken this example, with some personal emendations, from the fascinating study of Proust by Roger Shattuck, *Proust's Binoculars: A Study of Memory, Time, and Recognition in A la recherche du temps perdu* (London: Princeton University Press, 1964), 79–83.

41. For illuminating analysis of genre, see Mary Gerhart's forthcoming work entitled *Genre and Public Discourse*.
42. See "Style," in *Princeton Encyclopedia of Poetry and Poetics*, Ed. Alex Preminger (Princeton, NJ: Princeton University Press, 1965), 136–41.
43. See, for example, the work of Paul Ricoeur on the productive (as distinct from merely reproductive) imagination. For bibliography and analysis of the disputes on "text," see Werner Jeanrond's work, cited in n. 39.
44. Most theories of the imagination, it should be noted, are based on either perceptual rather than linguistic models (e.g., Sartre) or purely romantic and expressionist (e.g., Coleridge) or neo-Kantian (e.g., Gordon Kaufmann).

CHAPTER 3: RADICAL PLURALITY: THE QUESTION OF LANGUAGE

1. See Richard Rorty, ed., *The Linguistic Turn* (Chicago: University of Chicago, 1967).
2. In a lecture on the Vienna school at the 1983 University of Chicago seminar (with D. Tracy) on "Explanation and Understanding," thus far unpublished.
3. Ludwig Wittgenstein, as cited in Allen Thiher, *Words in Reflection: Modern Language Theory and Postmodern Fiction* (Chicago: University of Chicago Press, 1984), 13.
4. In the analytical tradition, see especially W. V. O. Quine, *From A Logical Point of View* (Cambridge, MA: Harvard University Press, 1953); Nelson Goodman, *Problems and Projects* (New York: Hackett, 1972); Hilary Putnam, *Mind, Language and Reality* (Cambridge: Cambridge University Press, 1975).
5. See George Lindbeck on the romantic-"expressivist" view of language—an acute analysis of the problem, even if some of his candidates for that position (e.g., Paul Ricoeur) are bizarre choices; see George Lindbeck, *The Nature of Doctrine: Religion and Theology in a Postliberal Age* (Philadelphia: Westminster, 1984), 136.
6. On the narrative character of such languages, see Alasdair MacIntyre's illuminating interpretations of the Homeric culture in *After Virtue: A Study in Moral Theory* (Notre Dame, IN: University of Notre Dame Press, 1981), 115–30, 169–74. For a second example, see the "shame-guilt" paradigm employed by E. R. Dodds in *The Greeks and the Irrational* (Berkeley and Los Angeles: University of California Press, 1951).
7. Recall Heidegger's analysis of "tools" in his early work in *Being and Time* (London: SCM, 1962) 91–145, an analysis still illuminating after he shifted his major interest, in his later work, to language itself.
8. The most radical proposal here remains Jacques Lacan's; inter alia, see *The Four Fundamental Concepts of Psychoanalysis* (New York: Norton, 1979); *Écrits: A Selection* (New York: Norton, 1977). For the category, see also Paul Ricoeur, *Freud and Philosophy: An Essay on Interpretation* (New Haven, CT: Yale University Press, 1970).
9. It should be recalled, however, that Protagoras's famous dictum had already been challenged in antiquity by Plato—especially in his late dialogues, where "God is the measure of all things." For a Christian theological challenge to a reigning anthropocentrism in theology itself, see James M. Gustafson, *Ethics in a Theocentric Perspective*, 2 vols. (Chicago: University of Chicago Press, 1983).
10. Hannah Arendt, *The Human Condition* (Chicago: University of Chicago Press, 1958), esp. 50–58; see also the collection for Arendt, Terence Ball, ed., *Political Theory and Praxis: New Perspectives* (Minneapolis: University of Minnesota Press, 1977); and Melvyn A. Hill, ed., *Hannah Arendt: The Recovery of the Public World* (New York, 1979).

11. See George Steiner's generous and critical assessment of Heidegger here in *Martin Heidegger* (New York: Viking, 1979), esp. 127–58. See also Karsten Harries, "Heidegger as a Political Thinker" in *Heidegger and Modern Philosophy*, ed. Michael Murray (New Haven, CT: Yale University Press, 1978), 304–29.

12. Ludwig Wittgenstein, *On Certainty* (New York: Harper Torchbooks, 1969), esp. 9–22.

13. This is true not only of *Being and Time* but implicitly, but no less genuinely, of the latter reflections on language and being; note, for example, the historicity of the analysis in *The Question Concerning Technology and Other Essays* (New York: Garland, 1977), 3–36.

14. On "publicness" see *Being and Time*, 210–25; on calculative and meditative thought, see *Basic Writings*, ed. D. Krell (New York: Harper & Row, 1977), esp. 319–93, and the essays in *Poetry, Language, Thought* (New York: Harper & Row, 1971).

15. It is here, perhaps, that Heidegger remains Derrida's chief mentor—even given Derrida's reservations on Heidegger on "difference." See, inter alia, Martin Heidegger, *Identity and Difference* (New York: Harper & Row, 1969). See also Jacques Derrida, *Margins of Philosophy* (Chicago: University of Chicago, 1982), 1–69; *Spurs: Nietzsche's Style*, (Chicago: University of Chicago Press, 1978) 114–22; *Of Grammatology*, (Baltimore: Johns Hopkins University Press, 1974) 18–26. Note here the illuminating analysis of Heidegger, Wittgenstein, Saussure, and the question of "postmodernity" in the already-cited Allen Thiher, *Words in Reflection: Modern Language Theory and Postmodern Fiction*. I acknowledge with gratitude that Thiher's analysis has influenced some of my formulations on the "postmodern."

16. Allen Thiher, *Words in Reflection: Modern Language Theory and Postmodern Fiction* (Chicago, 1984).

17. The locus classicus which has occasioned paradoxical difficulties not only of interpretation but even of the proper text remains Ferdinand de Saussure, *Course in General Linguistics*, trans. Wade Baskin (New York: McGraw-Hill, 1966). For interpretations see Allen Thiher, *Words in Reflection*, 63–91; Terry Eagleton, *Literary Theory*, 96–110; Jonathan Culler, *Ferdinand de Saussure* (London: Penguin, 1976).

18. For examples, see Umberto Eco, *A Theory of Semiotics* (Bloomington, IN: Indiana University Press, 1976); Terence Hawkes, *Structuralism and Semiotics* (Berkeley and Los Angeles: University of California Press, 1977); Richard Macksey and Eugenio Donato, eds.), *The Structuralist Controversy: The Languages of Criticism and the Sciences of Man* (Baltimore: Johns Hopkins University Press, 1972).

19. Paul Ricoeur, *Interpretation Theory: Discourse and the Surplus of Meaning* (Fort Worth, TX: Texas Christian University Press, 1976). See also the analysis of French conflicts on "discourse" in Diane Macdonell, *Theories of Discourse: An Introduction* (New York: Blackwell, 1986).

20. Emile Benveniste, *Problèmes de linguistique générale* (Paris: Gallimard, 1966).

21. The debates here among experts occasion a proper hesitancy—especially given the character of the exact "text" of the various texts of Saussure's own work!

22. For this analysis, besides Saussure himself, note the works cited in n. 17. I should like to thank Katrina McLeod for helping me revise an earlier draft of this section on Saussure.

23. *Course in General Linguistics*, 120. The official English translation reads, "In language there are only differences."

24. Inter alia, see Claude Lévi-Strauss, *The Savage Mind* (Chicago: University of Chicago Press, 1966); *The Elementary Structures of Kinship* (Boston: Beacon Press, 1969); and the great four-volume work on mythologies.

25. Examples here include Lévi-Strauss, titles in n. 24; Roman Jakobson, *Main Trends*

in the Science of Language (London, 1973); Gérard Genette, *Narrative Discourse* (Oxford: Oxford University Press, 1980); Roland Barthes, *Writing Degree Zero and Elements of Semiology* (Boston: Beacon, 1953) and *S/Z* (New York: Hill and Wang, 1974).

26. Jacques Derrida, "Genesis and Structure," in *Writing and Difference* (Chicago: University of Chicago Press, 1978), 160.

27. On the rhetoric of the topics, see the citations in chap. 2, n. 8; on a radically destabilizing rhetoric of the tropes, see Paul de Man, *Blindness and Insight: Essays in the Rhetoric of Contemporary Criticism* (Oxford: Oxford University Press, 1971) and *Allegories of Reading: Figural Language in Rousseau, Nietzsche, Rilke and Proust* (New Haven, CT: Yale University Press, 1979).

28. For a clear example of this attack on hierarchies, see the attack on the "oppositional" method of dialectical thought and its hierarchical character (e.g., through sublation of differences) in Gilles Deleuze, *Nietzsche and Philosophy* (New York: Columbia University Press, 1983), 147–95. In Derrida himself, see esp. (on Hegel and Genet) *Glas* (Baltimore: John Hopkins University Press, 1981).

29. On Saussure, see *On Grammatology* (Baltimore: Johns Hopkins Press, 1974), 35–71; on Lévi-Strauss, ibid., 95–269.

30. The category "dissemination," which emerges after *Grammatology*, seems to me the most radical of Derrida's categories; see *Dissemination* (Chicago: University of Chicago Press, 1981).

31. That Plato ever held such a position of pure presence seems to me untrue—or true only by ignoring the subtlety of the dialogues (not only the later ones like *Timaeus*, which seem to insist, by their use of myth, on just the opposite of any idea of pure self-presence, but even the *Phaedrus* and the *Republic*). For Derrida on Husserl, see *Speech and Phenomena, and Other Essays on Husserl's Theory of Signs* (Evanston, IL: Northwestern University Press, 1973).

32. See Susan Handelman, *The Slayers of Moses: The Emergence of Rabbinic Interpretation in Modern Literary Theory* (Albany, NY: State University of New York Press, 1982), for suggestive analyses of Derrida's possible use of rabbinic practices to challenge the "Greeks" and "Christians" (the latter two would hardly recognize themselves in Handelman's portrait). Nonetheless, her suggestion of how the traditional Jewish-Greek debate may be resurfacing in new ways is illuminating; and not only in Harold Bloom's explicit reworking of the conflict in literary theory (see *Kabbalah and Criticism* [New York: Seabury, 1975]) but also in Derrida himself, as when he writes (of Joyce), "And what is the legitimacy, what is the meaning of the copula in this proposition from perhaps the most Hegelian of modern novelists; Jewgreek is greekjew. Extremes meet?", in "Violence and Metaphysics," in *Writing and Difference*, 153. See also the essays in Mark Krupnick, ed., *Displacement: Derrida and After* (Bloomington, IN: Indiana University Press, 1983).

33. See Jacques Derrida, *La Carte postale: de Socrates à Freud et au-delà* (Paris, 1980), and on *pharmakon* see "Plato's Pharmacy," in *Dissemination*. On these and related issues, I wish to express my thanks to Françoise Meltzer.

34. This is also the reason why those thinkers (like Habermas) who defend some kind of transcendental analysis of communication make their case not on the basis of any transcendental philosophy of consciousness but on an analysis of discourse. There remain, of course, significant differences between positions like Derrida's and those like Habermas's; but those differences cannot be judged as if they were debates over traditional philosophies of consciousness and contemporary philosophies of language. See Jürgen Habermas, *Der philosophische Diskurs der Moderne* (Frankfurt am Main: Suhrkamp Verlag, 1985), esp. 191–248 (on Derrida) and 279–313 (on Foucault); the essay on Heidegger, on the other

hand, is somewhat bizarre 158–91; for a "new-French" analysis of Habermas, see Jean-François Lyotard *The Post-Modern Condition: A Report on Knowledge* (Minneapolis: University of Minnesota Press, 1984), 60–73.

35. Derrida, "Structure, Sign and Play in the Discourse of the Human Sciences," in *Writing and Difference*, 278–90.

36. For an interesting comparison of Derrida and Nargarjuna, see Robert Magliola, *Derrida on the Mend* (West Lafayette, IN: Purdue University Press, 1984). For an illuminating study of the similarities and differences of Derrida and Wittgenstein, see Henry Staten, *Wittgenstein and Derrida* (Lincoln: University of Nebraska Press, 1984).

37. For one hermeneutical response to Derrida, see Paul Ricoeur, *The Rule of Metaphor*, (Toronto: University of Toronto Press, 1977) 8th study; for a second, see David Hoy, "Decoding Derrida," *London Review of Books* 4, 3 (Feb. 1982): 3–5; and "Jacques Derrida," in Quentin Skinner, ed., *The Return of Grand Theory in the Human Sciences* (Cambridge: Cambridge University Press, 1985), 41–65.

38. Such an argument seems to be the basic thrust of, for example, Habermas to Derrida as mentioned in n. 34. Such arguments are important but must also deal explicitly with the radical rhetorical-linguistic issues Derrida raises for all such analyses. On rhetorical grounds, the conflict seems to become increasingly one between a rhetoric of reasonable *topics* and radically destabilizing *tropes*.

39. These seem to be especially the case in secondary works like the influential survey analyses of Jonathan Culler, e.g., *On Deconstruction: Theory and Criticism after Structuralism* (Ithaca, NY: Cornell University Press, 1982). A more interesting philosophical case can be found in Christopher Norris, *Contest of Faculties: Philosophy and Theory after Deconstruction* (London: Methuen, 1985).

40. Derrida's point, of course, is that certain words can undo the claim to unity in a text—as in the undecidability of Rousseau's use of the word *supplément* in his *Essay on the Origins of Language*. The analysis of Paul de Man on Rousseau-Derrida is interesting here; see the Rousseau section in his *Allegories of Reading*. See also Derrida's interpretation of Lacan's interpretation of Poe's *A Purloined Letter*, as well as Barbara Johnson's interpretation of Derrida-Lacan-Poe in Barbara Johnson, "The Frame of Reference: Poe, Lacan, Derrida," in *The Critical Difference: Essays in the Contemporary Rhetoric of Reading* (Baltimore: Johns Hopkins Press, 1980). Derrida's major interest seems to be in textuality; one, but only one, of his major strategies is to locate those undecidable words (like *supplément*) or phrases (like Nietzsche's *"I forgot my umbrella"*) that call into question any claims to unity in a text while releasing the disseminating power of textuality. For the American debate on textuality, see William V. Spanos, Paul A. Boyé, and Daniel O'Hara eds., *The Question of Textuality: Strategies of Reading* (Bloomington, IN: Indiana University Press, 1982).

41. See Jacques Derrida, "Edmond Jabès and the Question of the Book," in *Writing and Difference*, 64–78. See also the study of Jabès by Susan Shapiro in her forthcoming book on a rhetorical and theological study of post-Shoah Jewish literature, philosophy, and theology.

42. See, for example, Paul Ricoeur, *Interpretation Theory*.

43. See Mikhail Bakhtin, *Problems of Dostoevsky's Poetics*, ed. Caryl Emerson (Minneapolis: University of Minnesota Press, 1984). See also Bakhtin's helpful complication of "dialogue" and "ideology" in what might be called a "discourse" direction in *The Dialogical Imagination: Four Essays by M. M. Bakhtin* (Austin, TX: University of Texas Press, 1981).

44. As I trust is clear, there is no consensus among the disparate thinkers listed as discourse analysts here. Consider, for example, the differences between Foucault's analysis of "anonymous discourses" and the positions of Ricoeur or Benveniste or yet again Bakhtin or Booth, or the differences of any one of them

from Habermas or Apel, or the differences of Habermas or Apel from Toulmin or Kuhn. The point, in sum, is not to claim the unity of a position but of a set of issues and a basically hermeneutical set of concerns that pervades the different methods and conclusions of those otherwise very different and sometimes mutually contradictory "discourse analysts." Besides the works of Foucault, Lacan, Benveniste, and Ricoeur already cited, see also Julia Kristeva, *Desire in Language* (New York: Columbia University Press, 1980) and *Powers of Horror* (New York: Columbia University Press, 1982); Frederic Jameson, *The Political Unconscious: Narrative as a Socially Symbolic Act* (Ithaca, NY: Cornell University Press, 1980) and *The Prison House of Language* (Princeton, NJ: Princeton University Press, 1972); Terry Eagleton, *Against the Grain* (London: Verso, 1986); Edward W. Said, *The World, the Text and the Critic* (Cambridge, MA: Harvard University Press, 1983); Michel de Certeau, *Heterologies: Discourse on the Other* (Minneapolis: University of Minnesota Press, 1986). For the general term "discourse" in some of its uses, see Diane Macdonell, *Theories of Discourse;* Antony Easthope, *Poetry as Discourse* (London: Methuen, 1983); John Rajchaan and Cornel West, eds., *Post-Analytic Philosophy* (New York: Columbia University Press, 1985).

45. For one example of this kind of analysis, see the work of Richard Rorty, which radicalizes the holistic "positions" in Quine-Sellars in an explicitly rhetorical direction, in *Philosophy and the Mirror of Nature* (Princeton, NJ: Princeton University Press, 1979).

46. See Paul Ricoeur, *The Rule of Metaphor* (Toronto: University of Toronto Press, 1977) and *Time and Narrative*, 3 vols.

47. See Michel Foucault, *The Order of Things: An Archaeology of the Human Sciences* (New York: Vintage, 1970); on Foucault's methods, see Hubert Dreyfus and Paul Rabinow, *Michel Foucault: Beyond Structuralism and Hermeneutics* (Chicago: University of Chicago Press, 1982); Mark Cousins and Athar Hussain, *Michel Foucault* (New York: St. Martin's Press, 1984).

48. Jacques Lacan, *Écrits* (Paris: Seuil, 1966). The English translation is as difficult and resistant as the original—properly so. On Lacan, see Shoshana Felman, "The Originality of Jacques Lacan," in *Poetics Today* 2, 16 (1980–81): 45–57; Joseph H. Smith and William Kerrigan, eds., *Interpreting Lacan* (New Haven, CT: Yale University Press, 1983); John P. Muller and William J. Richardson, *Lacan and Language: A Reader's Guide to Écrits* (New York: International Universities Press, 1982); Jane Gallop, *Reading Lacan* (Ithaca, NY: Cornell University Press, 1985).

49. See the arguments with de Man of Frank Lentricchia, *After the New Criticism* (Chicago: University of Chicago Press, 1980), 282–318.

50. Roland Barthes, *The Pleasure of the Text* (New York: Hill and Wang, 1974).

51. See Frank Lentricchia's retrieval of Kenneth Burke's notion of language as symbolic action here in *Criticism and Social Change* (Chicago: University of Chicago Press, 1983). In terms of the present chapter, Lentricchia's call is for "discourse"—as Kenneth Burke's might be said to have been all along. On Burke, see William H. Ruechert, *Kenneth Burke and the Drama of Human Relations* (Berkeley and Los Angeles: University of California Press, 1982).

CHAPTER 4: RADICAL AMBIGUITY: THE QUESTION OF HISTORY

1. See the study of Raymond Williams, *Keywords: A Vocabulary of Culture and Society* (New York: Oxford University Press, 1976).

2. This seems to me a major difficulty with Gadamer's approach to those traditions

to which we belong. One need not deny this actuality of tradition nor resist the never-ending need to appropriate the undeniable goods and truths of our traditions as *traditio,* not mere *tradita.* But we do need further strategies, intellectual and practical, for criticizing and suspecting the tradition as well—in this sense the Enlightenment heritage must be defended and appropriated, critically but no less really than other moments in the tradition. Above all, we need to realize that our options on participating or not participating in the traditions are not exhausted by the reified categories "liberalism" and "conservatism" any more than they are by "Enlightenment become scientism" and "a respect for tradition become romanticism or neoconservatism." The reality of our history is far more complex and ambiguous than any of these familiar options suggest: so too must be the intellectual and practical strategies for appropriating and criticizing all the traditions to which we "belong." My own work, I believe, has "participated in" the same kind of difficulties of reception of any "revisionary" proposals: the book entitled *Blessed Rage for Order* has often been "received" as more purely liberal than the revisionary model of the text itself, while *The Analogical Imagination*'s defense of classics and tradition within the revisionary model has sometimes been received as, in effect, a neo-conservative tract. There are, to be sure, problems in each text; but a careful reading of them does not lend itself to interpreting the "revisionary models" for fundamental and systematic theology presented there as either purely liberal Enlightenment or purely traditional. Perhaps the difficulty is partly occasioned by the dominant, but by no means exclusive, concern of those books with pluralism, whereas the need to examine both plurality and ambiguity and those together is the greater need for understanding culturally and theologically both our "situation" and the Christian tradition. I hope to return to this issue in relationship to the Christian tradition in a companion volume to this study.

3. As quoted in Nancy Mitford, *Madame de Pompadour* (New York: Harper & Row, 1970), 249.

4. Recall how Foucault's study, *Discipline and Punish* (London: Allen Lane, 1977) begins with Damien's execution, only to show how later modes of discipline and punishment, although less strictly corporeal, are nonetheless shocking in their move from body to mind.

5. William Blake, "The Chimney Sweeper," from *Songs of Innocence,* in *The Complete Poetry and Prose of William Blake* (Berkeley and Los Angeles: University of California Press, 1982).

6. For the best study here, and a persuasive analysis for the need for the new theological language of the *tremendum* for this event, see Arthur Cohen, *The Tremendum: A Theological Interpretation of the Holocaust* (New York: Crossroads, 1981).

7. See George Steiner, *Language and Silence* (New York: Atheneum, 1977), 3–95.

8. See the use of this category in Walter Benjamin, "Theses on the Philosophy of History," in *Illuminations* (New York: Schocken, 1968), and Johann Baptist Metz, *Faith in History and Society* (New York: Crossroads, 1980). A study of the appropriateness of the category for Jewish and Christian theology in facing the *tremendum* may be found in Elisabeth Schüssler Fiorenza and David Tracy, eds., *The Holocaust as Event of Interruption, Concilium* 175 (1984). I have tried to address some of the hermeneutical and Christian theological import of the *tremendum* in an article in a volume on the question, Irving Greenberg and Alvin Rosenfeld, eds. (Indiana University Press, forthcoming). See the important contributions there by Harold Bloom, Irving Greenberg, Emil Fackenheim, et al., as well as the work of Susan Shapiro in her hermeneutical and theological study of Jewish responses (forthcoming). I wish to express my thanks to Susan Shapiro, Steven Kepnes, and Joseph Edelheit for helping me begin to reflect on these issues.

9. The classic study on the hybris of Athens remains, of course, that of the great Athenian Thucydides, *The Peloponnesian War* (New York: Penguin, 1954). See especially his accounts of the debate on Melos and the defeat at Syracuse. For a recent scholarly study, see Alvin W. Gouldner, *Enter Plato: Classical Greece and the Origins of Social Theory* (New York: Basic Books, 1965).

10. For an excellent study, see David Grene, *Reality and the Heroic Pattern* (Chicago: University of Chicago Press, 1967).

11. The need to find ways to relate these "isms" explicitly and systemically may be found in Rosemary Radford Ruether, *Sexism and God-Talk: Toward a Feminist Theology* (Boston: Beacon, 1983).

12. See Elisabeth Schüssler Fiorenza, "A Feminist Biblical Hermeneutics: Biblical Interpretation and Liberation Theology," in *The Challenge of Liberation Theology: A First-World Response*, ed. L. Dale Richesin and Brian Mahan (Maryknoll, NY: Orbis, 1981); Letty M. Russell, ed., *Feminist Interpretation of the Bible* (Philadelphia: Westminster, 1985); Phyllis Trible, *God and the Rhetoric of Sexuality* (Philadelphia: Fortress, 1978).

13. See Rosemary Radford Ruether, *Faith and Fratricide: The Theological Roots of Anti-Semitism* (Minneapolis, MN: Winston Press, 1974): Charlotte Klein, *Anti-Judaism in Christian Theology* (Philadelphia: Fortress, 1975).

14. The principal emphasis of this work is, to repeat, on the plurality and ambiguity of receptions; on the productive side, see Janet Wolff, *The Social Production of Art* (London: Macmillan, 1981); Ernst Bloch et al., *Aesthetics and Politics* (New York: Schocken, 1977); Janet Wolff, *Aesthetics and the Sociology of Art* (London: George Allen and Unwin, 1983).

15. Ambiguity can mean, cognitively, the true and the false; morally, the good and the evil; religiously, the holy and the demonic.

16. See the interesting case studies in Richard Johnson et al., eds., *Making Histories: Studies in History Writing and Politics* (Minneapolis: University of Minnesota Press, 1982), and Paul Veyne, *Writing History* (Middletown, CT: Wesleyan University Press, 1984).

17. See Allen Thiher, *Words in Reflection* (Chicago: University of Chicago Press, 1985), 156–227.

18. Examples of some of the ways suggested here are W. B. Gallie, *Philosophy and the Historical Understanding* (New York: Schocken, 1964); Raymond Aron, *Introduction to the Philosophy of History: An Essay on the Limits of Historical Objectivity* (London: Weidenfeld and Nicolson, 1961); Marc Bloch, *The Historian's Craft* (New York: Random, 1953); Jacques Le Goff and Pierre Norc, eds., *Faire de l'histoire* (Paris, 1974): Patrick Gardiner, *The Nature of Historical Explanation* (Oxford: Oxford University Press, 1952); W. H. Dray, *Laws and Explanations in History* (Westport, CN: Greenword, 1957); Alfred Schmidt, *History and Structure: An Essay on Hegelian-Marxist and Structuralist Theories of History* (Cambridge, MA: MIT Press, 1981); as well as the illuminating work of Paul Ricoeur in *Time and Narrative*, 1:91–231; David Carr, *Phenomenology and the Problem of History* (Evanston, IL: Northwestern University Press, 1974).

19. See Emmanuel Le Roy Ladurie, *The Peasants of Languedoc* (Urbana, IL: University of Illinois Press, 1974); W. Jackson Bate, *Samuel Johnson* (New York: Harcourt, Brace, Jovanovich, 1975).

20. For example, Elisabeth Schüssler Fiorenza, *In Memory of Her: A Feminist Theological Reconstruction of Christian Origins* (New York: Crossroad, 1983); M. Z. Rosaldo and L. Lamphere, eds., *Women, Culture and Society* (Stanford, CA: Stanford University Press, 1974); S. McConnell-Ginet, R. Barker, and N. Furman, eds., *Women and Language in Literature and Society* (New York: Praeger, 1980); Elaine Marks and Isabelle de Courtwren, eds., *New French Feminisms* (Amherst,

MA: Schocken, 1979); "Writing and Sexual Difference," *Critical Inquiry*, vol 8, 2 (1981).

21. See Michel de Certeau, *Heterologies: Discourse on the Other* (Minneapolis: University of Minnesota Press, 1986); Tzvetan Todorov, *The Conquest of America* (New York: Harper & Row, 1984) The *Annales* school, in one sense, can be said to radicalize this archaeology of the other by their accounts of the importance of those ultimate nonhuman others, climate and geography; see the great work by Ferdinand Braudel, *The Mediterranean and the Mediterranean World in the Age of Philip II*, 2 vols. (New York: Harper & Row, 1972–73).

22. George Rudé, *The Crowd in the French Revolution* (Oxford: Oxford University Press, 1939); Eugene Genovese, *Roll Jordan Roll: The World the Slaves Made* (New York: Random, 1976); John Boswell, *Christianity, Social Tolerance, and Homosexuality* (Chicago: University of Chicago Press, 1980); Frances Yates, *The Rosicrucian Enlightenment* (Boston: Routledge and Kegan Paul, 1972).

23. See Arnoldo Momigliano, inter alia, *Alien Wisdom: The Limits of Hellenization* (Cambridge: Cambridge University Press, 1975); Hans Blumenberg, *The Legitimacy of the Modern Age* (Cambridge, MA: MIT Press, 1983).

24. Involved in this search is the need to recover the notion "tradition"; see the magisterial work Edward Shils, *Tradition* (Chicago: University of Chicago Press, 1981).

25. See Georg Lukacs on the realistic novel in *Studies in European Realism* (New York: Grosset and Dunlap, 1964) and *The Meaning of Contemporary Realism* (London: Merlin Press, 1963).

26. It may bear repeating that the present work may be complemented and possibly corrected by the kind of social theory available from Marx, Weber, and Durkheim through Habermas. For example, see Jürgen Habermas, *The Theory of Communicative Action*, vol. 1 (Boston: MIT Press, 1984); *Theorie des kommunikativen Handelns* 2 (Frankfurt, 1981); Anthony Giddens, *Central Problems in Social Theory: Action, Structure and Contradiction in Social Analysis* (Berkeley and Los Angeles: University of California Press, 1979) *The Constitution of Society* (Cambridge: Cambridge University Press, 1984); Edward Shils, *Center and Periphery: Essays in Microsociology* (Chicago: University of Chicago Press, 1975).

27. See Habermas's analysis of the contribution and limitations of both Weber's analysis of rationalization and Marx's notion of materialist dialectic, in *Theory of Communicative Action*, vol. 1. For the debate on Habermas, besides the works cited earlier, also see Garbis Kortian, *Metacritique* (Cambridge: Cambridge University Press, 1980); Richard J. Bernstein, *The Restructuring of Social and Political Theory* (New York: Harcourt, Brace, Jovanovich, 1976); John B. Thompson and David Held, eds., *Habermas: Critical Debates* (Cambridge, MA: MIT Press, 1982).

28. Inter alia, see Lewis Mumford, *Art and Technics* (New York: Columbia University Press, 1964) and *The Myth of the Machine* (New York: Harcourt, Brace, Jovanovich, 1967). See also Teresa de Lauretis, Andreas Huyssen, Kathleen Woodward, eds., *The Technological Imagination: Theories and Fictions* (Madison, WI: Coda Press, 1980); K. Woodward, ed., *The Myths of Information: Technology and Post-Industrial Culture* (Madison, WI: Coda Press, 1980). I wish to express my thanks here to the Aspen Institute for my participation in a 1984 seminar on the new technological revolutions and to James Buchanan for his reflections.

29. For the term, see Paul Ricoeur, *Freud and Philosophy* (New Haven, CT: Yale University Press, 1970), 32–36.

30. For example, see the work of Jean Piaget on cognitive development, e.g., *Psychology and Epistemology; Towards a Theory of Knowledge* (New York: Orion Press, 1971); note also the work of Lawrence Kohlberg on moral development, *The Psychology of Moral Development*, (New York: Harper & Row, 1983). But note also the important correctives to Kohlberg available in Carol Gilligan, *In a Different*

Voice (Cambridge, MA: Harvard University Press, 1982); James Fowler, *Becoming Adult, Becoming Christian: Adult Development and Christian Faith* (San Francisco: Harper & Row, 1984).

31. The notions of the self vary widely in the religions, of course, ranging from the analysis of the responsibility of the self in the great monotheistic religions (see H. R. Niebuhr, *Radical Monotheism and Western Culture* [New York: Harper & Row, 1960]) to the self-as-illusion in much Eastern, especially Hindu and Buddhist, thought. Amidst a vast literature, see the representative "The Status of the Individual in Mahayana Buddhist Philosophy," in Charles A. Moore, ed., *The Japanese Mind* (Honolulu, HI: Universty of Hawaii Press, 1967). For recent theological analyses of the contributions and ambiguities of Western monotheistic notions see Claude Geffré and Jean-Pierre Jossua, eds., *Monotheism, Concilium* 177 (1985).

32. The classic work here, for Western Christianity, remains Augustine; see especially his dialectic of the self in *The Confessions* and his yet more radical envisionment of human sin in his later anti-Pelagian works. In the modern period, Pascal and Kierkegaard remain the classic texts. Insofar as Dostoyevsky can be understood as representative of Eastern Orthodox Christianity, the same kind of Augustinian sense enters Eastern Christianity—although the genius of the latter is not Augustinian (but indeed often anti-Augustinian)—with a profound analysis of the human relationship to the cosmos rather than the Western dialectic of the self-in-history. In that sense, one may hope that Eastern Orthodoxy could provide a place where the Augustinian concerns of Western Christianity on the self and the cosmic concerns of Buddhism and Hinduism may find some new dialectic—as in the magisterial work of Mircea Eliade (see, for example, *Cosmos and History: The Myth of the Eternal Return* [Princeton, NJ: Princeton University Press, 1954]). For the modern Western analyses and developments of the Augustinian tradition, see Paul Ricoeur, *The Symbolism of Evil* (Boston: Beacon, 1967); Langdon Gilkey, *Reaping the Whirlwind: A Christian Interpretation of History* (New York: Crossroads, 1976). For an analysis of the dilemmas of the "self" in modern literature, see Robert Jones, "Confessing Our Selves," *Commonweal* 112 (1985): 305–7.

33. I refer here to the classical theological discussions of "justification" and "sanctification." The reading I give, I acknowledge, is a Catholic one—as, perhaps, were Schleiermacher's and Wesley's!

34. Amidst the vast literature here, see Stephen Beyer, *The Buddhist Experience: Sources and Interpretations* (Encino, CA: Dickenson, 1974); Edward Conze, *Buddhist Thought in India* (Ann Arbor, MI: University of Michigan Press, 1962); Kenneth Ch'en, *The Chinese Transformation of Buddhism* (Princeton, NJ: Princeton University Press, 1973); Mircea Eliade, *Yoga: Immortality and Freedom* (Princeton, NJ: Princeton University Press, 1958); Wendy Doniger O'Flaherty, *The Origins of Evil in Hindu Mythology* (Berkeley and Los Angeles: University of California Press, 1976) and *Dreams, Illusions and Other Realities* (Chicago: University of Chicago Press, 1984).

35. The debates on the concepts "rationality," "modernity," and "postmodernity" are central here; recall the Lyotard-Habermas conflict noted above, as well as Martin Hollis and Steven Lukes, eds., *Rationality and Relativism* (Cambridge, MA: MIT Press, 1982).

36. Friedrich Nietzsche, as cited in the essay "Nietzsche and the Idea of Metaphor," Malcomb Palsey, ed., *Nietzsche: Imagery and Thought* (Berkeley and Los Angeles: University of California Press, 1978), 70.

37. For the ambiguity intended in the text, see the analysis of the positive contribution of Marxist ideology critique in Bill Schwarz, ed., *On Ideology* (London, 1977). For a good analysis, see Alvin Gouldner, *The Dialectic of Ideology and Tech-*

nology: The Origins, Grammar and Future of Ideology (New York: Seabury, 1976). For an important alternative analysis of the Marxist traditions and their "hard" problems, see the work of Leszek Kolakowski, especially his masterful *Main Currents of Marxism*, 3 vols, (Oxford: Oxford University Press, 1978), esp. vol. 3, *The Breakdown;* see also Shlomo Avineri, ed., *Varieties of Marxism* (The Hague: Martinus Nijhoff, 1977); for an anti-Marxist reading, see Dante Germino, *Beyond Ideology* (Chicago: University of Chicago Press, 1967).

38. Those "material" conditions need not include, of course, only economic realities, but also physical (e.g., climatic), biological, and demographic and social realities—as any full theory of a "materialist dialectic" or, alternatively, a naturalistic pragmatism must allow and even demand. Dewey and Marx, on this reading, despite their otherwise vital differences, can both be read as attempting full (i.e., either dialectical or pragmatic-naturalist materialist) positions. For a valuable Christian theological reading of "materialism," see Nicholas Lash, *A Matter of Hope: A Theologian's Reflection on the Thought of Karl Marx* (Notre Dame, IN: University of Notre Dame Press, 1982).

39. See Genevieve Lloyd, *The Man of Reason: "Male" and "Female" in Western Philosophy* (Minneapolis: University of Minnesota Press, 1984); and Jean B. Elshtain, *Public Man, Private Woman: Women in Social and Political Thought* (Princeton, NJ: Princeton University Press, 1981).

40. This is the major problem for myself in some of my own earlier formulations of the achievements of a phenomenological-transcendental analysis in *Blessed Rage for Order* (New York: Seabury, 1975) 43–64. To abandon that optimistic appraisal is not to abandon the demand for such transcendental analysis— whether linguistically and sociologically and analogically informed discourse analysis like that of Habermas or the necessarily metaphysical character of theological claims as in Hartshorne. In sum, the need to reformulate all earlier transcendental analyses which are based on a philosophy of consciousness seems clear and difficult. The need, however, to demand that kind of analysis for all the implicit validity claims in all our discourse and, even more so, for the logically unique claims of theology on the strictly necessary individual, God, seems equally clear. Lonergan's insistence that his version of "transcendental method" should not be interpreted in a neo-Kantian way but as a "generalized empirical method" is also relevant here.

41. I use the phrases *modernity* and *postmodernity* here as cultural descriptions: my own evaluation of postmodernity, as I trust the text makes clear, does not lend itself to that other version of "postmodernity," viz., neoconservatism. On the latter phenomenon, see Peter Steinfels, *The Neo-Conservatives* (New York: Simon and Schuster, 1979); on the possibly neoconservative character (despite their clear intentions) of postmodern French thought, see Jürgen Habermas, *Der philosophische Diskurs der Moderne* (Frankfurt: Suhrkamp Verlag, 1985), esp. 65–191.

42. This remains true, as suggested in the prior discussion of Derrida, whenever there is a reluctance, occasioned by radical reflections on language, to analyze the ethical-political consequences of one's position.

43. For the category, see, inter alia, Roland Barthes, *Image, Music, Text* (New York: Hill and Wang, 1979).

44. Stanley Fish, *Is There a Text in This Class?* (Cambridge, MA: Harvard University Press, 1980).

45. Michel Foucault, *Power, Truth, Strategy*, ed. Meaghan Morris and Paul Patton (Sydney: Feral Publications, 1979), and *Power/Knowledge*, ed. C. Gordon (New York: Panteon, 1972).

46. Besides the works already cited, see Michel Foucault, *Madness and Civilization* (New York: Random House, 1965); *The Birth of the Clinic* (London: Tavistock,

1973); *The Use of Pleasure: The History of Sexuality*, vol. 2 (New York: Pantheon, 1985).

47. Examples of the positions cited here are the works of Eliade, Foucault, Lacan, Todorov, de Certeau, and Kristeva already cited. See also Maurice Blanchot, *The Writing of the Disaster* (Lincoln: University of Nebraska Press, 1986); Georges Bataille, *Visions of Excess* (Minneapolis: University of Minnesota Press, 1985).

48. The debate on the use of the example of psychoanalysis by the Frankfurt school both to clarify the psychoanalytical concept of "systemic distortion" as repression and to develop the category for use in social-cultural analysis remains important here; see the debates in Richard J. Bernstein, ed., *Habermas and Modernity* (Cambridge, MA: MIT Press, 1985). Habermas's more recent turn to the developmental theories of Piaget and Kohlberg seem to me, despite some clarificatory gains, a retreat on the earlier Frankfurt school's (and the early Habermas's) more explicitly psychoanalytical model. See also Barnaby B. Barratt, *Psychic Reality and Psychoanalytic Knowing* (Hillsdale, NJ: Analytic Press, 1984). I wish to express my thanks here to Mary Knutsen for her important work on these issues; she is presently completing a dissertation on these issues in the context of feminist theory. I also wish to thank Francoise Meltzer, Bernard Rubin, and Charles Elder for helping me read and possibly understand some of the crucial texts of Lacan—who is, I believe, the most radical and most important of the contemporary French interpreters of Freud, as well as the best critic of much revisionary Freudianism, especially in the United States.

49. An analytical analysis of the category may be found in Raymond Geuss, *The Idea of Critical Theory* (Cambridge: Cambridge University Press, 1981); a more explicitly hermeneutical and historical account may be found in Rick Roderick, *Habermas and the Foundations of Critical Theory* (New York: St. Martin's Press, 1986).

50. This is not to say, as many still do, that Aristotle had no historical sense at all: a curious charge toward a thinker whose most typical strategy is first to review the opinions on the question and (especially in his natural scientific works and his political work) to attempt an empirical and implicitly historical test-case approach (e.g., on the various historical constitutions in Greece). That Aristotle did not possess modern historical methods and postmodern senses of radical plurality and ambiguity is, of course, clear; that he possessed, however, a "dogmatic" and "ahistorical" method is a fiction that cannot survive a reading of his works.

51. Adorno's acknowledgment, to be sure, was the most partial and pessimistic of all—especially in his notion of a purely "negative dialectics" in *Negative Dialectics* (New York: Seabury, 1973). His use (like those of Benjamin, Horkheimer, Marcuse, et al.) of "internal criticism," however, is consistent with, but not identical to, his more pessimistic analysis of the availability of a purely negative dialectic. Note Geuss's approval of Adorno here and Habermas's difference from him. In Christian theology, the work of Jürgen Moltmann on a Christian ideology critique is especially valuable here. For a radical theological proposal on negative dialectics, analogous to Adorno's secular work, see Joseph Columbo's unpublished dissertation on "Negative Dialectics and Christian Theology" (Chicago, 1986). On Adorno, see Gillian Rose, *The Melancholy Science: An Introduction to the Thought of Theodor W. Adorno* (London: Macmillan, 1978); Susan Buck-Morss, *The Origin of Negative Dialectics* (Brighton, MA: Harvester Press, 1977).

52. The most important work to date on this issue is Richard Bernstein's important retrievals of phronesis in the contemporary context; see especially *Beyond Objectivism and Relativism: Science, Hermeneutics, and Praxis* (Philadelphia: University of Pennsylvania Press, 1983).

CHAPTER 5: RESISTANCE AND HOPE: THE QUESTION OF RELIGION

1. See Michel Foucault, *The Order of Things: An Archaeology of the Human Sciences* (New York: Vintage, 1970), 387.
2. For a defense of this dialectic of the emergence of the need to defend a de-centered but genuine subject, see Paul Ricoeur, *Freud and Philosophy: An Essay on Interpretation* (New Haven, CT: Yale University Press, 1970), 419–94. See also Hilary Lawson, *Reflexivity: The Post-Modern Predicament* (LaSalle, IL: Open Court, 1985); Michael E. Zimmerman, *Eclipse of the Self: The Development of Heidegger's Concept of Authenticity* (Athens, OH: Ohio University Press, 1982).
3. See Peter Berger, *The Sacred Canopy: Elements of a Sociological Theory of Religion* (New York: Doubleday, 1967).
4. The work of the Niebuhrs remains exemplary here. See, for example, H. R. Niebuhr, *The Kingdom of God in America* (New York: Harper & Row, 1959); Reinhold Niebuhr, *The Irony of American History* (New York: Scribners, 1962); Reinhold Niebuhr, *The Nature and Destiny of Man*, 2 vols. (New York: Scribners, 1964).
5. See James M. Gustafson, *Ethics from a Theocentric Perspective*, vol. I (Chicago: University of Chicago Press, 1981), esp. 115–57, 235–81.
6. On the "aesthetic" see Hans-Georg Gadamer, *Truth and Method*, (New York: Crossroads, 1975), 5–80. For an important new study, see Jean-Pierre Jossua, *Pour une histoire religieuse de l'expérience littéraire* (Paris: du Cerf, 1985).
7. See Mircea Eliade, *Yoga, Immortality and Freedom* (Princeton, NJ: Princeton University Press, 1958), Joseph M. Kitagawa, *Religion in Japanese History* (New York, 1966), and Ioan P. Culiano, *Esperienze dell 'estasi dall 'Ellenismo Al Medioevo* (Roma Bari: Laterza, 1985).
8. In more technical terms, this can be formulated as a model of "mutually critical correlations" between interpretations of tradition and situation in the three sub-disciplines of fundamental, systematic, and practical theologies; for an expansion of this, see my analysis in *The Analogical Imagination* (New York: Crossroads, 1981), 47–99, or my more recent formulation in Hans Küng and David Tracy, *Theologie—Wohin? Auf den Weg zur einen neuer Paradigma* (Zurich: Benziger Verlag, 1984), 76–102.
9. On limit questions, see David Tracy, *Blessed Rage for Order* (New York: Seabury, 1975), 91–120.
10. For a comparative theological analysis here, see John B. Cobb, Jr., *Beyond Dialogue: Toward a Mutual Transformation of Christianity and Buddhism* (Philadelphia: Fortress, 1982).
11. See Richard Rorty, *Philosophy and the Mirror of Nature* (Princeton, NJ: Princeton University Press, 1979), 266–67.
12. The Whig histories often take the form of "social-evolutionary" theories that in either Comptean, Deweyan, or Habermasian forms seem to free the thinkers from much need to analyze the phenomena of religion and theology with the same care and acuteness as they analyze science, ethics, or art. For an insightful study of Dewey here, see William Shea, *The Naturalists and the Supernatural: Studies in Horizon and an American Philosophy of Religion* (Macon, GA: Mercer University Press, 1984).
13. For a persuasive theological "materialism," see Nicholas Lash, *A Matter of Hope: A Theologian's Reflections on the Thought of Karl Marx* (Notre Dame, IN: University of Notre Dame Press, 1981); on Heidegger and theology, see John D. Caputo, *Heidegger and Aquinas: An Essay on Overcoming Metaphysics* (New York: Fordham University Press, 1982).
14. To acknowledge the "crisis of ethical claims" as the most serious question for theologians today (as the feminist, political, and liberation theologians correctly insist) is not equivalent to displacing the still important (even for ethical political

analysis) "crisis of cognitive claims." The ethical-political and the strictly intellectual complexity of our pluralistic and ambiguous situation does not allow for such easy displacement—even by paradoxically theoretical accounts of the sublation of theory by praxis. Reinhold Niebuhr, for example, who insisted that the major crisis for theology was ethical-political, was nonetheless able to acknowledge the intellectual crisis as well—and learn from those, like Whitehead and Tillich, who concentrated most of their attention there. Similarly, theologians more concentrated on the intellectual crisis can clearly learn from the ethical-political analysis of the liberation and political theologians; for example, see Schubert Ogden, *Faith and Freedom: Toward a Theology of Liberation* (Nashville, TN: Abingdon, 1979); John Cobb, *Process Theology as Political Theology* (Philadelphia: Westminister, 1982); Roger Haight, *An Alternative Vision: an Interpretation of Liberation Theology* (New York: Paulist, 1985).

15. Here the work of Hans Küng and Edward Schillebeeckx and, more recently, Leonardo Boff and Juan Luis Segundo is exemplary; see, for example, Hans Küng, *Truthfulness: The Future of the Church* (London: Sheed and Ward, 1968); Edward Schillebeeckx, *Ministry* (New York: Crossroads, 1984); Jürgen Moltmann, *Hope for the Church*, ed. Theodore Runyon (Nashville, TN: Abingdon, 1979); Leonardo Boff, *Church, Charisma, Power: Liberation Theology and the Institutional Church* (New York: Crossroads, 1985); Juan Luis Segundo, *The Liberation of Theology* (Maryknoll, NY: Orbis, 1976); Juan Luis Segundo, *The Community Called Church* (Maryknoll, NY: Orbis, 1973); Rebecca S. Chopp, *The Praxis of Suffering: An Interpretation of Liberation and Political Theologies* (Maryknoll, NY: Orbis, 1986).

16. As cited in Richard John Neuhaus, *The Naked Public Square: Religion and Democracy in America* (Grand Rapids, MI: Eerdmans, 1984), 8.

17. See Schubert Ogden, *The Reality of God and Other Essays* (New York: Harper & Row, 1966).

18. The category "testimony" needs further reflection; for an important analysis, see Paul Ricoeur, "The Hermeneutics of Testimony," in *Essays on Biblical Interpretation*, ed. Lewis S. Mudge (Philadelphia: Fortress, 1980), 119–35.

19. See Ernst Bloch, *The Principle of Hope*, 3 vols. (Cambridge, MA: MIT Press, 1986). For a theological response to Bloch, see the works of Jürgen Moltmann, especially *Theology of Hope* (New York: Harper & Row, 1967) and also *The Crucified God* (New York: Harper & Row, 1973). The latter work is more like Adorno than Bloch: yet Moltmann, in his important and fascinating theological journey, has also returned more recently to Bloch for understanding creation.

20. See Mircea Eliade, *The Quest* (Chicago: University of Chicago Press, 1969).

21. See Michel Foucault on "scientia sexualis" in *The History of Sexuality*, vol. 1, *An Introduction* (Harmondsworth: Penguin, 1981).

22. An insistence on the use of the category "power" is one of the many strengths of the Reformed tradition of Christianity; for a succinct modern analysis of the Reformed "piety" appropriate to such an ultimate power bearing down upon us, see James M. Gustafson, *Ethics from a Theocentric Perspective*, vol. 1.

23. See several works by John Hick: *Problems of Religious Pluralism* (New York: Macmillan, 1985); *God Has Many Names* (Philadelphia: Westminster, 1980); *God and the Universe of Faiths* (New York: Macmillan, 1973); "Whatever Path Men Choose is Mine," in *Christianity and Other Religions*, ed. John Hick and Brian Hebblethwaite (Philadelphia; Fortress, 1980). For a study of Hick's work, see Chester Gillis's unpublished dissertation on Hick (Chicago, 1986).

24. See William James, *The Varieties of Religious Experience* (New York, 1982); see also Leszek Kolakowski, *Religion* (New York: Oxford University Press, 1982).

25. This is especially true of the pragmatists' insistence on the "community of inquiry"—most clearly formulated in the work of Charles Saunders Peirce.

26. If I recall correctly, I heard this happy observation first from Philip Blackwell.
27. I owe this observation to Eric Holzwarth; see his article on the question (forthcoming) and his dissertation on Barthes, Nabokov, and Woolf (Chicago, 1985). The latter, in revised form, is forthcoming as a book.
28. This is the suggestion of John Cobb, inter alia, in "The Religions," in *Christian Theology*, ed. Peter C. Hodgson and Robert H. King (Philadelphia: Fortress, 1982), 299–322. An alternative suggestion (based on a similar questioning of the category "religion") may be found in Wilfrid Cantwell Smith, *The Meaning and End of Religion* (New York: NAL, 1963) and *Towards a World Theology: Faith and the Comparative History of Religion* (Philadelphia: Westminster, 1980). Cobb's and Smith's critical reservations are well founded. One can, I hope, keep these reservations in mind while continuing to use the word *religion*—aware, one hopes, of its ambiguities but reluctant to abandon it until a better candidate than *ways* or *faiths* is coined.
29. If I may speak personally, I have learned the distinctiveness of Christianity not only from many books by Christian theologians on that subject but also by participation in Jewish-Christian and Buddhist-Christian dialogues. I have come to believe that only when those dialogues are taken seriously by all religious traditions can one fruitfully reopen traditional quests for the "essence" of Christianity or any other tradition. For similar suggestions, see Hans Küng, Josef von Ess, Heinrich von Streteneren, Heinz Bechert, *Christentum und Welt-Religion* (München: Hindler, 1984), 15–27, 617–25.
30. See my work, *The Analogical Imagination*, 446–57. See also the debates on "conceptual schemes" provoked by the article of Donald Davidson, "On the Very Idea of a Conceptual Scheme," in *Proceedings of the American Philosophical Association* 47 (1973–74); 5–20. The importance of this debate for religious studies may be seen in the work of Terry Godlove, "In What Sense Are Religions Conceptual Frameworks?" in *Journal of the American Academy of Religion* 52, 2 (1984): 289–305. That a Davidsonian position can also be developed into a fuller hermeneutical position where possibility and analogy would play the major conceptual roles continues to seem to me a promising alternative—both to the necessarily minimalist (but, I believe, correct) claims of Davidson and the possible confusions on these issues in the influential formulations of Clifford Geertz on "thick description" and "local knowledge"; for the latter, see Clifford Geertz, *Local Knowledge: Further Essays in Interpretive Anthropology* (New York: Basic Books, 1983), 53–73, 167–235.
31. For this reason there seems to me no need to go, in John Cobb's phrase, "beyond dialogue" to achieve mutual transformations—if the full demands of dialogue itself are realized; see John Cobb, *Beyond Dialogue*, 47–55. Also see Langdon Gilkey's essay, "The Mystery of Being and Nonbeing," in *Society and the Sacred* (New York: Crossroads, 1981).
32. See Harvey Cox, *Turning East* (New York: Simon and Schuster, 1977).
33. See the work of Western Buddhists such as Francis Cook, *The Jewel Net of Indra* (University Park, PA: Pennsylvania State University Press, 1978) and the forthcoming collection on Buddhist hermeneutics edited by Donald Lopez.
34. Aristotle was clearly a pluralist (and a good one, demanding criteria of relative adequacy for individual judgments on the best and for the most part) when dealing with matters that "could be other" (e.g., in dialectic and rhetoric in the *Topics*, in the *Rhetoric*, the *Ethics*, *Politics*, and *Poetics*); whether he was also one in the *Prior Analytic* or even in the *Metaphysics* remains an open question.
35. The debates among cultural anthropologists, as well as the use of "analogy" for historical judgments, are relevant here; see, for example, Harvey's discussion of analogy in Troeltsch et al. in *The Historian and the Believer* (New York: Macmillan, 1966) 15–19, 31–33, 90–99.

36. Surely Plato, in his use of the dramatic in his dialogues, recognized this; note the dramatic ways in which Socrates's interlocutors in the *Republic* force him to stay to converse only to find themselves (especially the youthful Glaucon and Adeimantus) led by the conversation to uncanny places where the hero of the drama, Socrates, replaces Achilles as the model for the good life for youth. For a close reading of these intricacies of the dialogue, see Allan Bloom, "Interpretive Essay," in *The Republic of Plato*, translated with notes and an interpretive essay by Allan Bloom (New York: Basic Books, 1968), 305–437.

37. See Thomas Merton, *The Asian Journal of Thomas Merton* (New York: New Directions, 1968); see also William Johnston, *The Still Point: Reflections on Zen and Christian Mysticism* (New York: Fordham University Press, 1971).

38. See, for example, John Cobb, *Beyond Dialogue*, 75–119.

39. See, for example, the important dialogical work of the Zen Buddhist thinker Masao Abe, e.g., "God, Emptiness and the True Self," and "Emptiness and Suchness," in *The Buddha Eye, An Anthology of the Kyoto School*, ed. Frederick Frank (New York: Crossroad, 1982), 61–74, 203–7. On Eckhart, see transl. and intro. Edmund Colledge, O.S.A. and Bernard McGinn, *Meister Eckhart: The Essential Sermons, Commentaries, Treatises, and Defense* (New York: Paulist, 1981).

40. Note the strategy suggested by George Rupp, *Beyond Existentialism and Zen: Religion in a Pluralistic World* (New York: Oxford University Press, 1979).

41. Ernst Troeltsch, "What Does 'Essence of Christianity' Mean?" in *Ernst Troeltsch: Writings on Theology and Religion*, ed. Robert Morgan and Michael Pye (Atlanta: John Knox Press, 1977), 124–80. A recognition of the greater ambiguity and plurality (both internal and "external") of Christianity since Troeltsch's essay provides further work for any post-Troeltschian attempt that desires basic fidelity to his ground-breaking enterprise. An important study of the hermeneutical complexity of contemporary theology may be found in Claude Geffré, *Le Christianisme Au risque de L'interprétation* (Paris: Du Cerf, 1983).

42. See Cornelia Dimmit and J. A. B. van Buitenen, eds., *Classical Hindu Mythology* (Philadelphia: Temple University Press, 1978); Ainslee L. Embree, ed., *The Hindu Tradition* (New York: Random, 1972); Wendy Doniger O'Flaherty, ed., *Hindu Myths: A Sourcebook* (New York: Penguin, 1975). This tradition of assimilation and plurality lived in classic modern form in Gandhi; see M. K. Gandhi, *An Autobiography of the Story of My Experiments with Truth*, 2 vols. (New York, 1929).

43. William James, *Varieties of Religious Experience*.

44. Recall, for example, the work of Martin Buber on the everyday. In Buber, see "The Question to the Single One," in *Between Man and Man* (London: Collins, 1961).

45. On the Latin American debate on "popular religion," see Segundo Galilea, "The Theology of Liberation and the Place of Folk Religion," in *Concilium What is Religion? An Enquiry for Christian Theology*, ed. Mircea Eliade and David Tracy (New York, 1980), 40–45. I wish to thank Mary McDonald and Tod Swanson, whose work in this and related areas is especially promising. Note also the similar kind of reflection on the ambiguity (not sheer negativity) of popular culture (e.g., the role of B-grade films) in the novels of Miguel Puig, such as *Betrayed by Rita Hayworth* (New York: Random House, 1981) and *Kiss of the Spider Woman* (New York: Random House, 1979).

46. I wish to express thanks to my colleague David Smigelskis, for his many helpful criticisms, including those on my own work's overemphasis on intensifications.

47. Those interpretations should, of course, include, even for theologians and philosophers, not only theological and philosophical interpretations of religion but all other important kinds of interpretation in the expanding field of religious studies. For example, here one often learns less about the distinctive religious resonances in Indian religious beliefs from philosophical-theological studies of

"Hindu thought" than from the exceptional interpretations of Indian myths, narratives, symbols, and beliefs in the work of Wendy Doniger O'Flaherty; besides those books already cited, see *Asceticism and Eroticism in the Mythology of Siva* (Oxford: Oxford University Press, 1973), *The Origins of Evil in Hindu Mythology* (Berkeley and Los Angeles: University of California Press, 1976), *Tales of Sex and Violence: Folklore, Sacrifice and Danger in the Jaiminiya Brahmana* (Chicago: University of Chicago Press, 1985).

48. This is not to claim that purely sociological or empirical-historical studies may not legitimately "bracket" the question of truth; but the fuller implications of these scholars' own work suggests that the "validity-claims" in religion, as in art, morality, and science, cannot be bracketed indefinitely for a relatively adequate interpretation of the phenomenon in question. The reciprocal work of historians of science and philosophers of science (like Kuhn and Toulmin,) suggests a more adequate model than the tendencies in some historians of art and of religion to hope that bracketing can work indefinitely. A collaborative model should be based on the *community* of inquiry—which contemporary religious studies could become. Such a community of inquiry (as distinct from warring fiefdoms) seems a more promising way forward for all scholars in religion.

49. The belief among many theologians that without "faith" and "belief" one cannot be a theologian remains as unpersuasive hermeneutically as it does theologically (faith is properly understood as gift, theology as task). The analogous notion that belief and faith disallow critical theology and scholarship is equally unpersuasive.

50. See the important methodological studies of Hans Penner here: inter alia, "The Fall and Rise of Methodology: A Retrospective Review," in *Religious Studies Review* 2, 1, (1976): 11–17; and (with Edward Yonan) "Is a Science of Religion Possible?" in *Journal of Religion* 52, 2 (1972); 107–34. In Christian theology, a recent methodological study is Francis Schüssler Fiorenza, *Foundational Theology, Jesus and the Church* (New York: Crossroads, 1984).

51. See especially Hans-Georg Gadamer, *Truth and Method*, 274–305. Gadamer's spectrum of application needs expansion; although, for example, both the theologian and the legal philosopher, like all interpreters, will need some application in order to understand, they will not need the same kind of application as the preacher and the judge. Similarly, as suggested in n. 48, other scholars (e.g., the historian of religion and the legal historian) will need their own kind of application and need not commit themselves to the fuller application of the theologian and legal philosopher, much less the preacher and the judge. That some application is needed seems clear; what kind is dependent upon the aim of the interpretation and methods and theories used to help fulfill that aim. Perhaps the model of "mutually critical correlations" for theology noted in n. 8, based as it is on the realization of the need for some application to interpret at all, might be used to clarify the kind of application needed for different kinds of interpretation across a whole range of possibilities. Perhaps it is also time for all scholars of religion to acknowledge that critical interpretations of the metaphor "bracketing" are as spent as literalist interpretations of the Scriptures. A careful analysis of what kind of application is implied by a particular task of interpretion could eliminate many unnecessary struggles between "block" or "wholesale" positions on "objectivity via bracketing" versus strictly "confessionalist" self-congratulations on their purity and communal self-identity.

52. The revival of interest in practical theology as the most demanding and complex theological task of all is relevant here; see Don S. Browning, ed., *Practical Theology: The Emerging Field in Theology, Church, and World* (New York: Harper & Row, 1983), and the constructive work in Dennis P. McCann and Charles R.

Strain, *Polity and Praxis: A Program for American Practical Theology* (Minneapolis: Winston-Seabury, 1985).

53. For a survey of some of the meanings here, see Claude Geffré and Gustavo Gutierrez eds., *The Mystical and Political Dimensions of the Christian Faith, Concilium* 96 (1974), and the frequent use of the phrase in the work of Johann Baptist Metz and Edward Schillebeeckx. Note also the implicit use of the category "mystical-political" in the great later works of Bernard Lonergan and Karl Rahner. Among Jewish theologians, note the use of Schelling in Arthur Cohen, *The Tremendum: A Theological Interpretation of the Holocaust* (New York: Crossroads, 1981). Note, too, the earlier work of Abraham Joshua Heschel. I hope to return to reflection on this option to try to clarify its fuller meaning for Christian theology in the companion volume to this work.

54. See Judith A. Berling, *The Syncretic Religion of Lin Chao-en* (New York: Columbia University Press, 1980); William de Bary and the Conference on Seventeenth-Century Chinese Thought, *The Unfolding of Neo-Confucianism* (New York: Columbia University Press, 1975); Julia Ching, *To Acquire Wisdom: The Way of Wang Yang-Ming* (New York: Columbia University Press, 1976); Anthony C. Yu, trans. and ed., *The Journey to the West*, 3 vols., (Chicago: University of Chicago Press, 1977–83); Wang Yang-Ming, *Instructions for Practical Living and Other Neo-Confucian Writings* (New York: Columbia University Press, 1963); as well as James Buchanan's forthcoming work on Taoist traditions.

55. A vast literature of examples exists: Roger Haight, *An Alternative Vision: An Interpretation of Liberation Theology* (New York: Paulist, 1985); Gustavo Gutierrez, *The Power of the Poor in History* (Maryknoll, NY: Orbis, 1981); Leonardo Boff, *Liberating Grace* (Maryknoll, NY: Orbis, 1979); Jon Sobrino, *Christology at the Crossroads* (Maryknoll, NY: Orbis, 1978); Matthew Lamb, *Solidarity With Victims: Toward a Theology of Social Transformation* (New York: Crossroads, 1982).

56. For this reason, I consider claims for the "hermeneutical privilege" of the poor ambiguous: that they are the "privileged ones" to God, yes; that they are the ones whose interpretations the rest of us most need to hear, yes (and a yes, which acknowledges the repression of those readings in past and present); that only those readings are "privileged" to be heard at all, clearly and firmly no (that claim is more fitting for Mao's Cultural Revolution than for serious, free, communal, and nonideological theological conversation and conflict).

57. See the books cited in n. 55 as well as Robert McAfee Brown, *Theology in a New Key: Responding to Liberation Themes* (Philadelphia: Westminster, 1978); Harvey Cox, *Religion in the Secular City* (New York: Simon and Schuster, 1984).

58. Albert Camus, "Why Spain?" (reply to Gabriel Marcel), in *Resistance, Rebellion and Death* (New York: Random House, 1969), 83.

59. See Richard Neuhaus, *The Naked Public Square*, (Grand Rapids, MI: Eerdmans, 1984) a valuable and civil study that merits serious reflection even by those, like myself, who do not agree with several of Neuhaus's neoconservative proposals but do agree with his central point in theologically defending the democracies. A similar agreement on the general point and serious disagreement with several of the details also applies to the "political" side of the theology of Wolfhart Pannenberg.

60. For examples of this, see the works cited in earlier notes.

61. For examples here, see the works of Metz, Moltmann, Radford Ruether, and E. Schüssler Fiorenza cited above. See also, James H. Cone, *God of the Oppressed* (New York: Seabury, 1975); Emil Fackenheim, *The Jewish Return into History* (New York: Schocken, 1978).

62. For two excellent examples of theology at its best in its sense of mystery, see Eberhard Jungel, *God as the Mystery of the World* (Grand Rapids, MI: Eerdmans,

1983), and Karl Rahner, *Foundations of Christian Faith: An Introduction the Idea of Christianity* (New York: Crossroads, 1978).

63. See Eberhard Bethge, *Bonhoeffer; Exile and Martyr* (New York: Seabury, 1975); Simone Pétrement, *Simone Weil* (New York: Pantheon, 1976).

64. See the debate here on clarifying this language by two leading process thinkers, Charles Hartshorne and Schubert Ogden, in *Existence and Actuality: Conversations with Charles Hartshorne*, ed. John B. Cobb and Franklin I. Gamwell (Chicago: University of Chicago Press, 1984), 16–43.

65. See Robert Bellah, Richard Madsen, William M. Sullivan, Ann Swidler and Steven M. Lipton, *Habits of the Heart: Individualism and Commitment in American Life* (Berkeley and Los Angeles: University of California, 1985); William M. Sullivan, *Reconstructing Public Philosophy* (Berkeley and Los Angeles: University of California, 1982).

66. Søren Kierkegaard, *Attack Upon Christendom* (Boston: Princeton University Press, 1954).

67. On the importance of mysticism for both philosophy and theology, see Louis Dupré, *The Other Dimension: A Search for the Meaning of Religious Attitudes* (New York: Doubleday, 1972).

68. The suggestion of a model of "friendship" with the text is developed by Wayne Booth in "The Way I Loved George Eliot: Friendship with Books as a Neglected Critical Metaphor," in *Kenyon Review* (1980), 4–27.

69. See the study of Steven Kepnes in his (to date unpublished) dissertation on Martin Buber on narrative (Chicago, 1983).

70. Contrast, for example, the two classic studies on the Greeks and reason: E. R. Dodds, *The Greeks and the Irrational* (Berkeley and Los Angeles: University of California, 1956), and Bruno Snell, *The Discovery of Mind: The Greek Origins of European Thought* (Oxford: Oxford University Press, 1953). For recent discussions, see Bryan Wilson, ed., *Rationality* (Oxford: Oxford University Press, 1970); S. Hollis and S. Lukes, eds., *Rationality and Relativism* (Oxford: Oxford University Press, 1982); Hilary Putnam, *Reason, Truth and History* (Cambridge: Cambridge University Press, 1981); T. Adorno and M. Horkheimer, *Dialectic of Enlightenment* (New York: Herder and Herder, 1972); Genevieve Lloyd, *The Man of Reason: "Male" and "Female" in Western Philosophy* (Minneapolis; University of Minnesota Press, 1984); Hans-Georg Gadamer, *Reason in the Age of Science* (Cambridge, MA: MIT Press, 1981).

71. This is not necessarily the case for all religious believers, of course, as Plato's attack on the "poets" and his insistence on the need for belief in the goodness of the gods for the polis suggests. Recall as well the terrifying portraits of the living God in much of Lamentations and Ecclesiastes. Also, Martin Luther's *deus nudus* remains a powerful Christian theological evocation of the terror often occasioned by God for Christians—and not only for Euripides' protagonists in the *Bacchae*. On "hope against hope," see the extraordinary book by Nadezhda Mandelstam, *Hope Against Hope: A Memoir* (New York: Atheneum, 1983).

72. I have tried to give some reasons for that trust in the books *Blessed Rage for Order* and *The Analogical Imagination*. Bibliography on the many works in this tradition may be found cited in those works.

Subject Index

Name Index